Archaeology

For Mikkel

Klavs Randsborg

Archaeology
and the Man-Made Material Reality

AARHUS UNIVERSITY PRESS

AARHUS UNIVERSITY PRESS
Building 170, Aarhus University
DK-8000 Aarhus C, Denmark

Preface

'cause they lived where I couldn't
we both asked the same
Why?

This slim volume came to life suddenly—*con amore*—in the summer of 1990, born during some transitional months and weeks, sometimes warm, sometimes chilly, when the balance of my various occupations was undergoing change and I was both consciously and unconsciously beginning to make plans for five challenging working years as a Research Professor in my old workplace, the Archaeological Institute of Copenhagen University – a challenge and a responsibility beyond what I had ever dreamt of. This meant that a number of duties acquired in my role as Professor at the University of Göteborg had to be shelved, very reluctantly, or else had to be accorded lesser importance. In this situation full of uncertainties, caught between duties and opportunities, I felt a need to have something concrete on which to concentrate, and that something developed into this little book, which I see, optimistically, as a 'mid-way testament', based on some twenty-five years of research, teaching and other experience of and in archaeology. I hope that it can prove of benefit to others besides myself.

The illustration-component is a very important part of what I hope will be an easily-read book; as in the case of many other archaeological works, it should be possible to grasp the book's message and evaluate it virtually by means of the illustrations alone. The illustration-captions thus make up the longest 'chapter' of the book. More detailed references to a number of phenomena and circumstances which are dealt with only briefly in the text can moreover be found in the annotated bibliography at the end of the book.

I owe thanks to so many people and institutions that I am at a loss to know where to begin or end. To put it as briefly as possible, I see my life—my dependence and my gratitude—unfolding in a span formed by impulses and interests in childhood and youth, by the Danish archaeological environment, and by the foreign countries which through the pleasure and enrichment of travelling and experiencing the new and strange were at first a revelation to me, and later a constant challenge, as well as a means of rediscovering freedom. The same applies to the people who have meant so much for my personal and intellectual development – between comfort and challenge.

It is perhaps easiest to think of this book as being written for students, maybe the day before the start of their studies, and for others with a similar background and interest in archaeology. The rather controversial contents should also, however, attract the curiosity of the more professional. The structure is thematic, and in contrast to most other introductions there are here no ambitions as to completeness or to presenting any single archaeological tradition—e.g. prehistoric or classical archaeology. The practical aspects of archaeology are only cursorily treated. On the other hand, I have allowed myself to concentrate on the important issues of the unity of archaeology and its great potential, and this gives the text a rather more personal tone. The examples used are by and large taken from Europe, the Mediterranean and the Near East – the area of my own experience.

This small written offering is dedicated to Mikkel, my very small son, and I can safely assume that he will view it in a light quite different from that in which I see it myself.

The text has been translated into English by Joan F. Davidson, who has faithfully interpreted my not always free-flowing pen; a number of drawings and figures are published with the kind permission of the Danish National Museum and other institutions.

Summer, 1990   *Klavs Randsborg*

Contents

Illustrations

Cover: The Bronze Age female grave from Skrydstrup, Denmark. From Randsborg 1984.
Back cover: Excavation of the huge sacrificial deposit of military equipment from c. AD 200 in Illerup bog, Denmark. Photo by Jørgen Ilkjær.

ARCHAEOLOGY AND THE MAN-MADE MATERIAL REALITY

12. The Vorbasse settlement, Denmark; the fourth century AD. From Hvass 1986 *44*
13. The Vorbasse settlement, Denmark; around AD 800. From Hvass 1986 *46*
14. The Vorbasse settlement, Denmark; the eleventh century AD. From Hvass 1986 *47*
15. Rocca San Silvestro (Italy); a medieval village. After Francovich & Parenti 1987 *49*
16. Settlement development in an area of Mesopotamia. Based on Adams 1981 *51*
17. Bronze placed in male and female Bronze Age graves in Denmark. From Randsborg 1974 *56*
18. The Gudme-Lundeborg area, Denmark; a royal centre and emporium. Based on Randsborg 1990 (II) with additions *61*
19. City-planning in the late first millennium BC at Olynth, Greece. From Hoepfner & Schwander 1986 *63*
20. Carving on a Bronze Age stone cist at Kivik, Sweden. Cf. Randsborg 1990 (I); photo Riksantikvarieämbetet, Stockholm *67*
21. Imported ceramics from the first millennium BC in southern France. From Randsborg 1989 (III) *70*
22. Church-building in Constantinople (Istanbul) up to AD 1453. From Randsborg 1991 based on Müller-Wiener 1977 *73*
23. Prehistoric (Iron Age) cemeteries in southern Sweden. From Hyenstrand 1979 *76*
24. Fjäle, Gotland (Sweden); the recorded archaeological landscape. From Carlsson 1989 *78*
25. Fjäle, Gotland (Sweden); the actual archaeological landscape. From Carlsson 1989 *79*
26. Columns from Constantinople displayed in Venice, Italy. Author's photograph *84*
27. Columns from the Jesus Church, Copenhagen, Denmark. Author's photograph *87*

Fig. 1. Excavation of a late Bronze Age ritual structure at Sandagergård, Sjælland (Zealand); Denmark, found during a systematic archaeological survey in connection with the construction of a gas pipeline.

The photo shows a number of the typical aspects of archaeological fieldwork today: 1) the excavation of settlements, whose often faint traces earlier research had great difficulties in recognizing; 2) the large scale of the approach, which includes archaeological surveys and the stripping off of the top-soil of large areas to expose traces of structures and various other constructions (e.g. fences and refuse-pits); and 3) the rôle of legislation and concomitant funding and administration in archaeological work, in the present example the statutes pertaining to the protection of ancient monuments and the organization of work in the cases where excavations have to be carried out before the construction of buildings, motorways, gas pipelines etc.

1. Archaeology

That which hath been is now; and that
which is to be hath already been; ...
(Ecclesiastes 3: 15)

This little book is both personal and impersonal; it is being written against a background of many conflicting emotions. One minute you find yourself aiming to survey your own experience and that of others, and to condense out what archaeology is in terms as objective as possible; the next minute you find you are only thinking of what has meant the most to you personally, and describing that. Sometimes we cut out all that is unimportant and think only of 'official' matters, and sometimes the personal experiences pour out, and your thoughts turn to what we ourselves have experienced—and how. How archaeology, from being an object, became the subject itself, and how one experienced it as a way of considering the world, so that it again became the object; how we see it now as the study of what you would call the man-made material reality, from the earliest times and up to today.

For most people, archaeology is synonymous with excavations of old graves, settlement-remains, perhaps even ruins, wrecks or treasure-hoards (fig. 1). The stuff of archaeology—or source material—according to this view, is old and as a rule it disappeared from the surface of the earth long ago. It has to be rediscovered, restored and reconstructed with the help of archaeologists. The archaeologist is thus a mixture of craftsman and prophet, who evaluates what is found and compares it with other finds—ordering, dating and creating images of vanished cultures and societies (cf. fig. 2).

But does this make the entire archaeological reality?

We feel relatively certain that a well-polished, wedge-shaped flint object from a Stone-Age grave is in fact—and *was* in fact—an axe blade. But the technical analogies soon begin to fail us, and we are compelled to stray further from them in order to understand and explain. If the axe is found in a grave, it should not just be seen as a tool, but also as an object which reflects a series of relations between the living and the then newly-dead in the specific region and period of human history in question. The axe is here a feature of a situation, a context. Suddenly it is not just a testimony about a certain technology and some simple economic and cultural conditions; it has become a symbol of the society and ideology of a distant age. If the axe is compared with other stone axes, in other graves and in other finds, we can thus build up a taxonomy which is comprised of a more and more complete hierarchy of images of what we call the past.

But it is one thing to legitimize archaeology with regard to other disciplines and to vindicate it externally in relation to the modern world's colossal range of observations and experiences. It is quite another matter to experience archaeological reality as I myself, and perhaps others, have done. In terms of practical work you may classify and compare limited groups of archaeological source-material, e.g. the flint axes already mentioned. But first and foremost you are looking for *patterns*—I often use the term 'structures'—in all of this chaotic source-material. Things and their contexts are my materials; my means consist of knowledge about human life. And the final results—what are they?

In one sense these results are concrete, and in another they are not. In fact, we presuppose that a number of the patterns or structures we see mean something—often something specific. This we have to do; this is after all the way we communicate. But we also know that our observations can change from one day to another, in spite of all the efforts we have made in drawing comparisons and in particular in trying to make the observations match. In this way our reality—that of our archaeological, scientific results—is both present and elusive. Perhaps in the last analysis the only thing we know is our own archaeological reality.

At the same time, however, you are not alone in the world; you take colour from your surroundings—your present and your past—and share, to a greater or lesser extent, the experiences of others, e.g. a conception of what it is to practise archaeology. I, like you, therefore alternate between the personal and the non-personal, i.e. the official academic view.

ARCHAEOLOGY AND THE MAN-MADE MATERIAL REALITY

Fig. 2. Gilded brooch of bronze from a female grave at Nørre Sandegård on the island of Bornholm, Denmark; seventh century AD. The fibula is decorated with two antithetical, backward-looking animals whose enlarged hind thighs and legs are intertwined and whose jaws are biting their own double-outlined body as well as the hind foot. The thighs also form the mask of a bearded man which, seen upside down, resembles a doubled-up and bound human figure. An interesting piece of so-called Germanic animal ornamentation.

This photo shows a classic fascination of archaeology, the encounter with foreign artefacts which may have the added interest of belonging to the past of one's own country or home region. The artefact is an expression of past technologies, trade in raw materials, organization of production and society and—as is immediately evident from the appearance of the item—of a culture and ideology rooted in an alien historical tradition.

The 'objective' view, however, is not without problems. Modern archaeology since the last century has energetically developed the language and terms necessary to permit the handling of its subjects of study as unambiguously as possible. But this type of communication can also hinder understanding, e.g. by compressing phenomena into predetermined categories. The problem is that neither archaeology nor its source-material is in fact an independent, value-free entity.

I do not believe, therefore, that the practice of archaeology is purely a matter of bringing to light a source-material, taking care of it, and putting it into order. I do not believe that archaeology forms a delimited academic, or for that matter non-academic, field. And nor do I believe, therefore, that what we call archaeological source-material consists in itself of a closed universe, even if I also take every opportunity of asserting the value of the material and its particular qualities, e.g. in comparison with spoken and written language. But to question independence, objectivity and the accepted order is dangerous. It means creating chaos and insecurity; it means, in other words, challenging the social norms, no matter how innocent it may appear.

But what norms, what security, can I call into question?

Chaos, after all, is everywhere: in our uncertain understanding of the world around us, from the moment when we leave the familiar everyday certainties; chaos characterized the source-material which archaeology began to explore in the last century, and chaos reigns in the archaeological world today where understanding of the past is concerned. Chaos and uncertainty, in other words, are a central part of our archaeological cognition. Without constantly entering into chaos and seeking structures and creating meaning our understanding is merely repetitive or dead. In reality we are constantly engaged in bringing forward proposals to sort out chaos, while at the same time we keep abandoning the newly-created theories in favour of further explorations. The reader may well find this presentation rather too romantic, but is it not the real nature of cognition that it is constantly uncertain?

The fact that a concrete organisation of museums and university institutes has gradually been built up around archaeology and its source-material, along with the experience acquired so far and the practices immediately current, should not lead one to think of organisation in itself as being identical with cognition. Even an excavation in which new source-material is brought to light is not necessarily the same as the creation of new archaeological knowledge. This can only happen by what one might call venturing out into chaos and expanding the universe. An important step is taken, however, in the excavation process itself or in the course of any other means of isolating and observing part of the material reality. But that step is limited if it does not confirm, invalidate or in some other way relate to accepted convention, both in the form of the results that have been achieved and in the context in which they have been achieved.

The humanistic academic disciplines acquired their modern

form in the last century and were based, then as now, chiefly on investigations of human motives, language and communication, and transactions. The primary source-material—where it was not man himself—was written. The ideal form research took permitted the inclusion of certain aesthetic subjects, such as pictorial art, however, but treated as something purely marginal the ordinary results of human transactions—the man-made material reality.

Even human interplay with nature, or man's existence as a biological being, were not subjects of great interest to the early modern humanistic disciplines. Fixated on the written testimonies as the humanists were, the body and food were split off from the soul and handed to the medical and natural scientists—an example of classifications both advancing and holding back understanding. Those researchers, such as archaeologists, who were supposed to study the remains of the man-made material reality of distant times, constantly had to justify themselves to the academic world of that time; often they were not even seen as 'true' academics, but merely as caretakers of museum collections. Viewed in this perspective archaeology has had to develop in a long slow haul through dealing with a source-material—a segment of chaos—in opposition to the traditional norms and their cognitive and organisational forms.

Archaeology, however, has also itself set limits for its own activities, e.g. by only studying earth-found sources. The experience which has been acquired through time, the working methods which have been created in the attempt to see a larger world through the material, have not yet led to a systematic expansion of the universe of archaeology. So long as the archaeologists chiefly excavated, sorted, dated and compared finds, this was perhaps to be expected. But from the moment when the archaeological context—e.g. the grave with the flint axe—was recognized for what it is—a message about a prehistoric cultural and social pattern—a new situation came into being, and its consequences must necessarily embrace the totality.

From that moment onwards, the possibilities for archaeological cognition actually stretched to the horizons of man's existence, from the earliest times—if not earlier—up to our own present time, anywhere on the earth. At the same time it became possible to rewrite history, or rather to create a new history on the basis of the material sources. These can be found, at any rate in principle, for all ages and all areas, independently of written and other forms of evidence, criss-crossing societies. The whole world became the potential research field of archaeology, and its material is colossal, the questions legion. Only history, what actually happened—no matter what the form of our knowledge—and the order in which it happened, can set limits.

And that, I believe, is where we stand today. In contrast to what we often believe ourselves, we have become masters of time, but not of material. We have created archaeology with all its museums and other institutions for e.g. looking after earth-finds, the remains of the distant past. But we have still not yet sufficiently realised that we can see the whole of man-made material reality as 'archaeology', that the material is a general 'principle'; that the concept of treating the world through the material, if this is not to put it in too bombastic terms, is a manifestation of life. Finally, the fact of dealing with and analysing the environment around oneself, the past and the present at the same time, is also the pre-condition for being able to develop the principles of the search which has to take place on the journey of exploration between source-material and chaos.

Archaeology, despite its tradition and in contrast to the character of the typical source-material, is contemporary. Professional history, or the tradition of the subject, takes account only of that quality of the finds which has dictated their ordering to date. It is in the present day that the departure-point of archaeology is situated; this gives it its justification and motivation, and determines which questions it is interesting to investigate with the source-material as the tangible, present challenge.

But chaos and uncertainty are also dispersed from the present, stimulated by our own searching. Archaeology, like many other forms of knowledge, therefore stands out in contrast to the familiar certainties—the predictable—which we try with all our strength to extend, through our economies and society, to cover the whole earth and all circumstances. Archaeology is therefore helping, in a manner of speaking, to ensure that chaos survives time, and that our understanding of the world is not finite.

2. The Object and Its Time

..., seeking traces,
I picked up this arrow, useless
with its broken point and
corroded cracks. ...
Li Ho (791-817)

Archaeology alternates between details and horizons. The focus sweeps from the object to the place and to the meaning: three concepts which are also the most important elements in the development of archaeology itself. The earliest archaeological efforts concentrated on objects; objects which were different from what one normally had in sight, objects which belonged to another age or another world: stone axes or Greek vases—the objects which made up the first collections of rare artefacts, the first museums, or which were displayed for ornament and not least to testify to their owner's broad geographical and spiritual—or so we were supposed to think—horizons.

The first question posed of an object was, and is: 'What is it?'; the second is, 'Where does it come from?', and the third is 'How old is it?'

The first question was often easy to answer, but in some cases it could be difficult. A wedge-shaped polished object of stone—is that in fact an axe? The second question was usually also easy to answer, so long as elementary information had been supplied with the object, or so long as it lent itself in some other way to having its place of origin identified. The last question, however, was as a rule difficult, except where coins were concerned, since these often bore a representation of known potentates; but how old is the stone axe, how old is the Greek vase, in fact?

Often the beginning of modern archaeology is dated to the moment when it began to be able to answer questions about the age of objects in a way which seems to us rational, from the moment at the beginning of the last century when a Stone, a

Bronze and an Iron Age became established realities e.g. in Denmark; or from the moment when the Greek vases became chronologically fixed in relation to each other and to the historical chronology known for instance from the classical writers. But this definition of the discipline of archaeology is possibly too narrow. It limits the field to the time when archaeology began to have a fixed organisation, primarily in the form of museums, and when international standards for archaeological studies began to be established in practice.

This would make archaeological thinking before around 1800 or 1850 uninteresting and reduce its practitioners almost to ignoramuses; and it is recognizably wrong. The early archaeological thinking was almost without presuppositions, but it was not stupid, and the early intellectual archaeology was undoubtedly a necessary precondition for the later work, quite in line with the establishment and maintenance of the first collections and museums which were opened in the early 19th century, and where one could enjoy the opportunity to test out one's academic hypotheses.

The fuel which raised sparks around the early-modern development of archaeological research was the rational interest in history which was further fed by the marked development of nation-states in the last century. In other academic disciplines in the humanities and in social sciences, in biology, geology, etc., similar systematic attempts were made to understand the main principles of the course of development, fundamental characteristics, etc. But behind these academic changes there undoubtedly also lay the development towards rationalism of the 'hard' and 'soft' natural sciences, and in particular their exploitation by early trade capitalism and especially, later, industrialism. In this way academic thought and study—originally coloured and conditioned by theology—came to become part of everyday rationality and of the practical knowledge about nature, products and human life which had accumulated throughout the millennia.

Evolutionist thinking, among other things, played an important role in archaeology, for instance in questions of how technology and trades developed. This was also the case within ethnography, where so-called primitive societies were regarded as the relics of a distant time, before the development of the states and civilisations which for instance formed the basis of Western Europe. Within biology and geology, the natural laws were adopted as overruling principles which could finally allow the account of Creation and the chronology of the Bible to be laid to rest. This had implications for archaeology also, planting the first idea that the so-called 'prehistoric period'—the time before the written sources and the civilisations—was not just a phenomenon which characterised peripheral regions such as Denmark, but the whole world. It was among other things the find of stone tools in layers together with extinct animal species which was decisive in this respect.

Within archaeology, one speaks of both a relative and an absolute chronology. The reason is that it is often easier to establish a chronological relationship between two objects, than it is to date either of those objects precisely. Even in the early 19th century, archaeologists made systematic observations of what objects were found, for instance, in the same grave, and therefore were contemporary, and of what graves, in a mound, were situated above or below others, and thus recorded the inherent testimony of the objects and the burial customs as to their relative chronology.

One of the earliest systems of relative chronology was based on a classification of the objects from prehistory into the same functional types—primarily tools and weapons—according to materials, in fact stone, bronze and iron. This classification was seen, from as early as the beginning of the last century, to mirror an order in time, a chronological sequence. The sequence was the famous three-period system, associated with the Danish archaeologist C.J. Thomsen, who in the middle of the last century was at the head of museum activities in Denmark (fig. 3). Thomsen collected a number of people around him who created the academic norms and the archaeological practice which became standard-setting for the development of what is known as prehistoric, or more accurately, general, archaeology. This area of archaeology could not seek support from written sources and was obliged from an early stage to create its own conceptual apparatus. In addition, the source-material was often relatively unimpressive, so that all

C. J. Thomsen i Oldnord. Museum
noa Christiansborg.

ARCHAEOLOGY AND THE MAN-MADE MATERIAL REALITY

aspects and methods had to be taken into consideration—hence the term 'general archaeology' used here.

Other archaeological research traditions also have roots in museum collections or private ones—often art collections—but e.g. for Near Eastern archaeology the fascination felt in the Victorian Age for the Biblical lands no doubt played the most significant role, along with influences from classical archaeology. For classical archaeology—the Nestor of archaeologies—on the other hand, it was the late 18th century's interest in the world of classical antiquity which had decisive significance. Moreover, the subject's earliest methodological development was shaped by another Dane—Georg Zoëga. The emergence of classical archaeology was thus not prompted by the nation-state, whose real development belongs to the 19th century, but by interest in the classical cultural heritage—e.g. the republican form of government and the Athenian democracy, which could be used as counter-images to late-feudal Europe in the dream about new conditions in society. Since then the bourgeoisie of industrialism has taken over the preoccupation with antiquity and appropriated it as one of its distinctive cultural symbols. What is more, the ruins from the Classical Age, justly admired since the Renaissance, constituted a conspicuous body of source-material which, like sculptures, vases, etc., eloquently invited art-historical and relative chronogical—or typological—studies.

The archaeological artefact-based chronology systems from the end of the last century were based either broadly on the three-

Fig. 3 (facing page). C. J. Thomsen—the 'father' of the three-age system—showing visitors round the Museum of Northern Antiquities ('National Museum') at Christiansborg Castle in 1846 (Drawing by M. Petersen).

This very correct, yet idealized drawing in the tradition of bourgeois art of the early nineteenth century shows the aged curator and a group of visitors to his museum. Popularization became an established feature of archaeological research and of the museums from an early stage. In the present case, it was directed towards the understanding of national antiquities, in others of the splendour of ancient Greece and Rome, or the 'foreignness' and fascination of things alien to Europe.

period system or on entirely different source-groups, e.g. settlement layers in Continental European caves which had been used by the hunters of the Ice Age. Often attempts were made to make the artefacts more-or-less themselves reveal the chronological sequence, e.g. by setting up sequences from the simple to the elaborate. These attempts were precarious on methodological grounds, but several of the relative chronological systems which were established were—and are—still convincing. This is true perhaps especially of the system devised by the Swede, O. Montelius, using six artefact-periods for the span of more than 1000 years in the Nordic Bronze Age. The truth is that a system such as the Montelian one was actually built upon criteria of contemporaneity, defined by the combinations of artefact-types found in graves and confirmed *inter alia* by isolated so-called stratigraphic observations made at burial-mound sites, i.e. observations of the relation between the times of construction of different graves within the same mound.

Observations of this type were conditional on the excavations or on controlled and systematic collection of information which gradually came to take place on a large scale. Towards the end of the last century the archaeological activities had freed themselves from the old collections with their predominantly singly-found objects. A new source-material was created on the foundation of the old, as were the principles for the exploration of that material.

In more recent times, studies of the relative chronology of artefacts has continued intensively, often assisted in the last few years by computer analyses, which make possible the rapid testing-out of hypotheses about connections and sequences. These investigations are based—as in Montelius's time—in virtually all cases on the so-called 'closed finds', i.e. combinations of objects of different types, e.g. from graves (cf. fig. 4).

The absolute chronology for the more distant periods of the past had until relatively recently to be established through comparisons with dated historical events, e.g. in the Roman Empire, in ancient Greece, or for yet more distant periods, Egypt, whose history can be followed in detail through written evidence for the last five thousand years. This was, and is, both an insecure and a laborious method which demands on the one hand that the

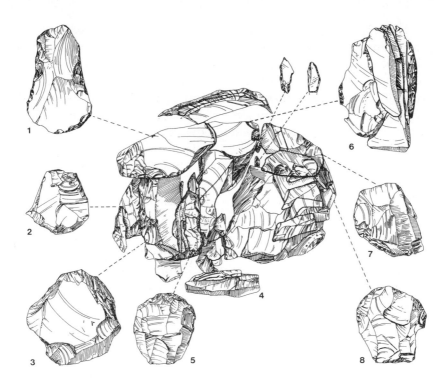

Fig. 4. 'Re-fitting' flint refuse and some tools from a Mesolithic (early Stone Age) settlement at Rørmyr (II), Høgnipen, southern Norway.

This simple, though time-consuming technique demonstrates the procedures of flint-knapping and at the same time solves major chronological problems on a site where there is no detailed stratigraphy or well-defined contexts for the ratefacts. A prerequisite for the technique is completeness of the excavation, a demand which only modern excavations of rather small settlements can fulfil.

relative chronology is well-developed in the areas from which bridges are to be built, e.g. the civilisations along the Mediterranean and in Egypt, and on the other that there are well-dated objects which are common to the areas and which can link them together in a fixed system. Such objects can be, for instance, items that were traded between the areas, or which were copied from area to area.

However simple these principles may sound, the realities are something quite different, and a trustworthy relative and absolute chronological system even for Europe after 3000 BC has not yet been achieved, either with traditional methods or with modern natural-science techniques. This is particularly true of the period before coins became common at the end of the first millennium BC. Moreover, no matter how advanced a traditionally constructed European chronology could become, it would never be possible either to link the American continents with it or those continents to the Egyptian Pharaoh sequence.

A chronological break-through for archaeological research came, however, with the C-14 method, which was developed after the Second World War, and which was based on the principle that radioactive matter is broken down and converted to normal matter of the same type. This happens at a known rate; for radio-active carbon, C-14, it takes 5730 years for just half of the matter to be broken down and converted to ordinary carbon. All living organisms contain both ordinary carbon and, in a stable ratio, small quantities of radioactive but non-dangerous carbon. When an organism, e.g. a tree, dies, the radioactive carbon is slowly broken down, and by measuring the quantity which is left in a sample, e.g. charcoal from an excavated fireplace, one can thus hope to date the fireplace and the objects which have been found in association with it. Such a method is completely independent of historical chronology, and even if it is not without complications it permits the dating, within certain tolerances, of archaeological and other material anywhere on the earth within the last 40,000 years or more (fig. 5).

An even more accurate method is what is known as dendro-chronology, which is based on the fact that growth-conditions for trees vary from year to year according to the weather situation, and this creates an identifiable pattern of year-rings in the wood. By establishing standard sequences, e.g. for oakwood from different growing-areas, archaeological samples, for instance wood from coffins, can be placed in time and—if the latest year-rings are included in the sample—it can even be possible to determine the exact date of felling of the tree.

The famous Bronze Age grave from Egtved in Jutland has been

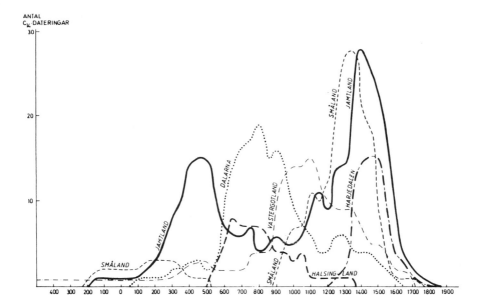

Fig. 5. C-14 dates of iron-production sites from various parts of Sweden.
The figure is a fine example of the great potential of the C-14 method. The iron-resources of the various regions were used in different periods. This raises interesting questions about the control and trade of iron, as well as the links with other relations of production and society. At the same time, the diagram illustrates the great potential of archaeology for historical studies, especially in periods without other sources.

dated by this method to the year 1370 BC, and this of course also applies to the objects which were found in the grave (fig. 6). By a process of comparing these objects with others the relative chronology of the Bronze Age in the Nordic region can thus be established—or in fact made absolute—without any need to take the long and uncertain route over the Continent and the Mediterranean to Egypt. Dendrochronology is without doubt by far the most precise of what are termed the natural-science dating methods which are known today, but it requires the establishment of securely-identified regional standard curves for the different species of tree, and also relatively large pieces of wood, preferably with of the order of 100 year-rings. In particular in the Mediterranean region, where there are few bogs to preserve old wood, this has proved to be a significant problem.

Nevertheless, there are reasons for optimism concerning this chronological work. Even if these studies are far from being complete, the new dating methods have resulted in the freeing of much energy for other types of investigative work. But before moving on to those, we should first evaluate a few of archaeology's basic qualities and its potential: what the man-made material world or reality can tell us about places and other geographical dimensions.

Fig. 6 (facing page). The Egtved oak-coffin grave from a Bronze Age mound in Jutland, Denmark. Dendro-chronologically dated to the year 1370 BC with exceptionally well-preserved organic materials. The body of a young woman (aged 16 to 18 years) is resting on a cowhide, dressed in a woollen string-skirt and a short woven woollen blouse; the belt is also woollen and woven. On the feet are pieces of woollen cloth. Covering the body was a woven blanket, likewise of wool. At the feet, there is a bucket made of birch-bark for mead; a box made from wood shavings, beside the head, contains a hairnet and an awl. An ornamented bronze plate of rather poor workmanship and a comb of horn can be seen at the belt; an arm-band and an arm-ring of bronze and one small ear-ring were also found. A bundle of woollen cloth at the lower left leg held the cremated bones of a child (aged 5-6 years). Finally, the coffin contained some remains of plants—including the flower of a milfoil, whose season is the period from June to September—insects, etc.

ARCHAEOLOGY AND THE MAN-MADE MATERIAL REALITY

3. The Place and the Context

I see humanity in twilight,
between past and future;
and in two dimensions,
time and place. ...
Abu al-Ala al-Ma'arri (973-1057)

In the earliest museums, or rather collections of artefacts, the find-places played only a very small role; it was the objects themselves that were considered important. Occasionally the find-place was known, and even perhaps the find-circumstances, but it was not until the early-modern, rational or systematic archaeology—the new methods and the resultant defined professional language—that interest arose in the find-place and the find-context, and that these conditions could be ascribed real significance.

As a rule the find-place is not just a place where an artefact or burial mound is located. Often other artefacts—mounds or other relics—are found, or have been found, at the same site. In other words, it is possible to establish a connection, a context, in which the finds can be placed, and which permits the study of chronological and other relationships. Is it not much more important to know that a collection of five artefacts of bronze comes from two graves, one of them constructed over the other in the same mound, objects 1-3 from the lower grave and nos. 4-5 from the upper one, than merely to have those objects displayed in their showcase? In this specific example, with its clear context, consideration of chronological, cultural, social and other aspects can be undertaken: the artefacts 1-3 and 4-5 respectively must be contemporary and must belong to the same cultural milieu, and nos. 1-3 must be older than 4-5. If the character of the objects permits it, or if there are discernible skeleton-remains in the graves, it may be possible to identify one of the graves as belonging to e.g. an adult man, and the other to a young woman (cf. fig. 6).

ARCHAEOLOGY AND THE MAN-MADE MATERIAL REALITY

The find-contexts need not, however, be limited to a specific grave or mound. Other contemporary, earlier or later finds from the area can give rise to a number of considerations, the nature of which we shall examine in the following chapter on the food-supply economy and settlements—the landscapes of archaeology. In early modern archaeology, however, and especially after the turn of the century, what knowledge of find-places was used for was to gain insight into the distribution of different types of ancient artefact and of cultural phenomena. These were phenomena which had been identified e.g. by means of chronological studies, and, with the help of geographical surveys, representations could now be put together of e.g. the most important cultural regions, as a rule completely without reference to the find-contexts.

In the latter part of the last century the question of find-context came to be recognised clearly as a precondition for chronological studies, and series of prehistoric periods with curious names such as Montelius period III (the Nordic Bronze Age) and the Dipylon Age (the Greek Iron Age) had been or were established, covering large parts of Europe and the Mediterranean basin. In a fashion which corresponded to the earlier search for distinctive chronological boundaries and structures in the archaeological material, now that the basic principles for chronological sequence had been established, attention gravitated towards the geographical differences and groupings which could be identified everywhere. For instance, artefacts of the so-called Nordic type from Montelius period III from the Bronze Age were found primarily in South Scandinavia and the northernmost part of Germany, and occurred only very rarely further south. In Central Europe the artefacts from the same phase, in spite of certain general similarities, were of other types, and south of the Alps the picture was again quite different.

It goes without saying that behind such interests there lay a knowledge of geographically structured or conditioned cultural differences which were often regarded as covering chronologically independent or stable cultural qualities, which ideally should be, and often were, found in their highest expression in the nation-state. Other driving forces in the research of the time were the desire to trace the peoples known from the classical writers, e.g.

the Germanic tribes, back in time—a desire which it was thought could be furthered by the study of the distinctive characteristics of the material culture, in spite of the chronological problems.

In 1925 the English archaeologist Gordon Childe put forward a now classic explanation of the cultural groupings, viz. that they represented groups within society, tribes, racial and possibly linguistic units. He expressed it on one occasion in this way (Childe 1925):

We find certain types of remains—pots, implements, ornaments, burial rites, house forms—constantly recurring together. Such a complex of regularly associated traits we shall term a 'cultural group' or just a 'culture'. We assume that such a complex is the material expression of what would today be called a 'people'. Only when the complex in question is regularly and exclusively associated with skeletal remains of a specific physical type would we venture to replace 'people' by the term 'race'.

Childe's explanatory model was alluring and attempted at one stroke to provide a method for further studies and an explanation of the structures which did as a matter of fact exist in the material. Today we know that there was no such thing as an identity of connection between material culture, society, language and physical types of humans, such as Childe was perhaps suggesting. Material culture is something one can 'participate in' no matter who one is otherwise, and it has its own development determined by traditions, contacts between societies, natural conditions and the 'long-wave' socio-economic course of history. But this does not mean that Childe and others had not pointed out an area of colossal and only partially-exploited potential within archaeology. Just as with the chronological conditions, however, it was even more difficult than many at first thought to find simple archaeological or historical 'natural laws' which explained the conditions one could observe in a cultural source-material. And often there was no coincidence of borders and cultural phenomena either, when one analysed them in greater detail.

Unfortunately many of these thoughts were taken up and used as part of chauvinistic social ideologies, e.g. Nazism, which saw itself as the heir of the Old Germanic societies: where the Germanic tribes once upon a time had had their Ur-home, the German-speaking peoples must also have the right to live, build and reign. The underlying idea was clearly that the world could be divided up into natural spheres of interest which had a historical basis. Strangely enough, this line of reasoning created a Slavonic counter-image, actually just as chauvinistic in character, which was built up by the Eastern European states after the Second World War. This ideological struggle, closely interwoven with the specific problems and expectations of the Communist countries, was the key to the release, among other things, of substantial resources for Slavonic archaeology, which thereby was granted the opportunity to carry out excavation projects on a scale which—for that time, and taking into account the general poverty of those societies—has to be considered massive. In fact settlement archaeology, among other subjects, acquired vital new impetus because of this development.

But no matter which ideologies have exploited, through the ages, the images of prehistoric cultural geography, these distribution-patterns are still a reality which presents a constant challenge to archaeological research. With the internationally-oriented academic and world perspectives of the present we thus have a tendency to see the cultural areas of history as a reflection of communication within the relevant area, where there must have been particularly close contacts at one or several points. We thus turn ourselves away from a naïve use of the older folk or tribe theories and 'translate' the archaeological culture areas into specific economic, social or ideological relations—listing those relations in random order. But an apparently orderly and objective view of this kind can actually also be wrong and may well underestimate the rôle which folk-groupings, migration of tribes, etc., may indeed have played in prehistoric times. We cannot reject 'ethnicity' as an important phenomenon just because the concept does not fit with modern Western (or Far Eastern) culture. Material culture can also be a way of expressing differences.

All this goes to show that we are faced with very complex problems, requiring us in our investigations to take into account both the older and the more recent, more 'technocratic', but still over-simplified or uni-dimensional archaeological models. We should rather go one step further and explain specific distributions of cultural features in geographical space—or e.g. in a particular context—as reflections of a correlation with respect to the feature in question. This correlation in a situation otherwise balanced probably also indicates common ideological norms. Phenomena or objects of the same type may well, however, occur in different contexts, for instance in cases of contacts between two very different societies; artefacts of different kinds can of course also have the same function in different contexts. Common features always imply, however, that the societies or social groups involved were in close contact with each other as regards the area of activity in question. Whether there were also other similarities, e.g. as regards the area of economics, has to be shown by closer analysis in each case.

It is easy to find examples in archaeological literature of modern, specific archaeological explanations of this type regarding geographically significant spreads of cultural elements. The occurrence of obsidian—a glass- or flint-like mineral—in the earliest agricultural cultures in the Middle East is such an example (fig. 7). Obsidian is a relatively rare raw material, much sought after in the Stone Age for shaping into tools. It is found naturally in the Near East, e.g. in some areas of Eastern Turkey. In the settlements near these regions of origin almost all the the stone tools were made of obsidian, and even three hundred kilometres from the 'mines' quite significant quantities of the raw material have been found, transported there by expeditions or through exchanges. More than 800 km. away from the places of origin obsidian is still found in the settlement sites, but only in very small quantities, no doubt exchanged over the large distance from small society to small society.

In this case it can therefore be seen that both technological-economical and social conditions lay behind the distribution of obsidian. Close to its origin the technological-economic considerations must have been dominant, but with an important basis in social relations. Further away, in areas where the raw material played only a lesser or very limited role in the local technology, the socially-related factors must have been decisive in its spread.

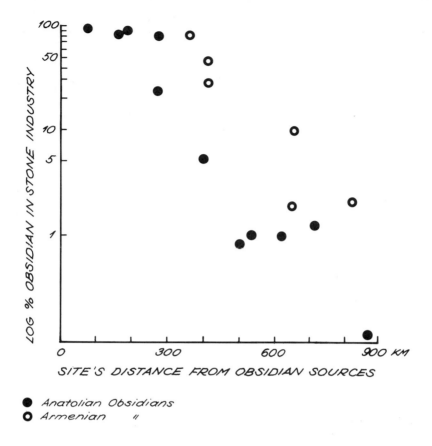

Fig. 7. Early neolithic agricultural settlements in the Near East from the seventh and sixth millennia BC. The diagram shows that the occurrence of tools made of obsidian (in proportion to those made of flint) decreases according to the distance from two distinct obsidian sources in eastern Turkey and neighbouring areas. Within a region of up to about 300 kilometres from the sources, however, the supply of obsidian is still abundant and nearly constant. This demonstrates the strength of the distribution systems and their different character, from being predominantly 'economical' (although no doubt socially rooted) in the large 'inner region' near the source, to being only 'social' in the outer one. In addition, the two obsidian-cources, although geographically quite near one another, have very different areas of distribution and diffusion, reflecting different social networks.

Common to the whole system, however, must have been a general recognition of the valued raw material—an 'obsidian-culture', on the lines of e.g. the value ascribed to Coca-Cola in both the developed and the less developed world today.

Another example of the modern observations and interpretations of geographically significant variations in distribution which can, however, be compared to the earlier interpretations of cultural differences, comes from Central Europe in the latter half of the first millennium AD (fig. 8). At that time there could be found, on either side of a quite distinct border running north-south, (approximately along the border between what used to be East and West Germany), two areas, each with its own building customs. To the west are found three-aisled long houses with two rows of posts supporting the roof; these long houses are the main buildings in rather large farmsteads. To the east are found groups of smaller pit- or block-houses sometimes connected to a castle-structure. In their main characteristics the natural conditions are, as is well-known, the same in the two areas, and the same plants are grown, the same animals kept and the same types of tools and weapons used, etc.

In a case such as this one might well first look for an explanation based on differences in the communications systems, probably with a background in both social structure and culture or ideology—at any rate in relation to norms for living-space. In this particular example, what we know in addition, however, is that the above-mentioned border corresponds closely to the dividing line between the Germanic and Slavonic societies respectively—each with its own language, as is shown e.g. by place-names—during the period in question. We cannot, however, wholly discard any of these hypotheses, but we must make different demands of the evidence before we can accept one or other interpretation, and we must specify precisely the various economic, social and cultural elements which enter into the classification of a phenomenon as either 'Germanic' or 'Slavonic'. And even then we cannot be certain about the nature of the link between the material systems we are faced with here and e.g. the linguistic or ideological conditions.

ARCHAEOLOGY AND THE MAN-MADE MATERIAL REALITY

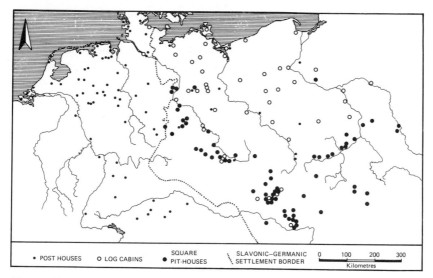

• POST HOUSES	○ LOG CABINS	SQUARE ● PIT-HOUSES	⋮ SLAVONIC–GERMANIC ⋮ SETTLEMENT BORDER	0 100 200 300
				Kilometres

Fig. 8. Dwellings in north Central Europe in the late first millennium AD. To the west the 'Germanic' so-called three-aisled houses with roof-bearing inner posts; to the east the 'Slavonic' log-cabins and (mainly in the lowlands) square pit-houses, respectively. Note also the border between Germanic and Slavonic place-names, etc.

In the last analysis, the material culture has its own autonomy. The structures we seek and recognise can only rarely be directly translated into phenomena we are familiar with from elsewhere; but does that make the structures less real? There is nothing to suggest that that is so. The difficulties lie rather in the area of communication between archaeologists and other professionals, or non-professionals, who are used to fixed definitions.

In addition there is of course the question of whether our traditional social and other categories are always as fixed as we normally believe them to be. The concept 'tribe', for example, has been shown in many cases to consist of a comfortable 'catch-all' which Roman officers or English colonial civil servants used of social groups they confronted in war or were required to administer, and to whom they needed to give an *ad hoc* name. Such names and terms later infiltrated into history, social anthropology and archaeology as fixed concepts.

More important than these terms and concepts, however, were the ordinary living conditions and the development of the settlement and of food production through the ordinary history of mankind—and these are significantly easier to handle archaeologically.

4. Landscapes and Living Conditions

> They dwell apart,
> dotted about here and there
> ... their villages are not laid out in
> the Roman style ...
> their food is plain ...
> Tacitus (*Germania* 16, 23), 98 AD

Since time and place are the two basic dimensions of all archaeological material, and in fact of all material, archaeology will always occupy itself with the local perspective; this is true most particularly of the conditions governing the context of the settlement and the provision of food, or the subsistence economy.

With their limited mobility, the people of the past, in spite of constant contacts with other societies, were totally dependent on local resources. This applies to any form of economy we may think of, from the first hunters and gatherers to the farmers of the 18th century, before industrialisation created the new market economy with large quantities of non-local products. Even today we are dependent on conditions such as resources and distances: we do not go further than necessary to obtain what we want.

Research into food supply economies is today an integrated and fully recognised part of all archaeological activities (figs. 9-10). There are, however, sectors of archaeology where until recently only minimal interest has been taken in the study of charred grain from settlements, broken fragments of animal bones from refuse heaps, or pollen diagrams (based on studies of flower-pollen) and their pictures of the vegetation of the past. For instance, it is only ten years ago that the first studies of food-waste from Ancient Rome, in that case animal bones, were carried out; and this in spite of the fact that thousands of excavations have taken place in that city in the last couple of hundred years. An example like this makes it clear how dependent archaeology is, not just on source material, but also on the practitioners' knowledge and priori-

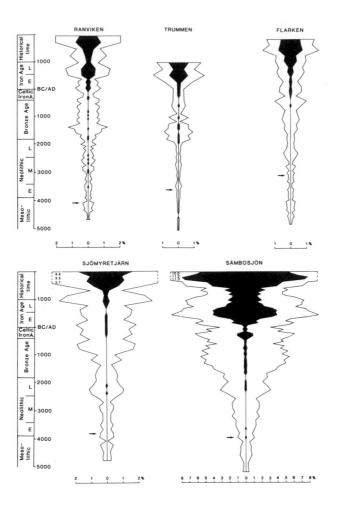

Fig. 9. So-called human-impact diagrams of the anthropogenic indicators among plants, based on pollen-analyses. Pollen from grain is marked with black; the first occurrence of plantain (indicating domesticated cattle) with arrows. The increase, over time, of the impact of man can be observed, but also some possible recessions. The localities are all in south-western Sweden, only Sämbosjön being in a prime agricultural area.

Such diagrams, though difficult to interpret, are very important in investigations of the character of subsistence conditions, and in comparative settlement-studies within a historical framework. One problem is that intensification of economic activity may not necessarily show in the diagram.

ARCHAEOLOGY AND THE MAN-MADE MATERIAL REALITY

ties—what they think it is important to concentrate on. In the Roman example the focus was on architecture and art.

Where early archaeology was concerned it was a problem even to find source material which could provide any certain information about the economy of the past, in that traces of food-supply or subsistence conditions are closely linked to rural settlements. Pollen analysis, which is based on identification and calculation of the pollen from the different earth-layers in bogs and similar areas, is a method which belongs to this century (fig. 9). It also presupposes that it is possible to date the individual layers, a precondition which as a rule was extremely difficult to meet before the development of the C-14 method after the Second World War.

All the same, there was a certain limited amount of settlement material available to early archaeologists such as the Danish circle gathered around the father of the three-period system, C.J. Thomsen (cf. fig. 3). In 1850 J.J.A. Worsaae, as a member of a commission for the study of oystershell-heaps, made the discovery that the shell-heaps were the piled-up refuse from meals, broken tools, etc., and were therefore in other words 'køkkenmøddinger' or kitchen middens; the Danish word from then on passed into international archaeological terminology. With recognition of this fact it all at once became possible to study what animals the hunters and gatherers of the time—for those were the occupations of the period in question—fed themselves on in the last centuries of the Mesolithic period—(the 'middle' Stone Age, or late Hunting Stone Age), before the introduction of agriculture in southern Scandinavia in the Neolithic period ('New' Stone Age, or Farming Stone Age).

In the second half of the last century many settlements were known, e.g. in the Mediterranean region, but the excavations there consisted mainly of uncovering architectural monuments and bringing ancient artefacts to light. It was only slowly that the general principles for taking measurements in three dimensions, exact studies of layer sequences in profiles across the excavation-field, etc., came to be adopted. In the temperate parts of Europe, especially beyond the areas of the old civilisations, stone buildings were virtually unknown in prehistory, and it therefore required significant excavation experience to be able to detect the traces of roof-bearing posts, lines of walls and other evidence which indicated the timber-built long-houses of the Iron Age—in spite of the large scale of these structures. It was easier to discern refuse layers and pits, whose dark, charcoal-blackened filling and high proportion of pot-sherds, etc., were relatively easy to pick out and which also often left traces on the surface of the soil.

From the animal bones in these refuse-layers and refuse-pits, from charred grain and impressions of grain in potsherds, etc., it was possible as early as the end of the last century to begin building up knowledge, in many places, of the nutrition or subsistence economy in the various periods of prehistory. With the introduction of pollen analysis towards the middle of this century further progress was made.

In parallel with this archaeological development, geologists, botanists and others had determined the general environmental conditions prevailing in these periods for many of the areas inhabited by mankind throughout the ages—at first, Africa, then the whole of the old world, and finally in Australia and the new world, which was the last part of the globe to be populated by man.

The geographical spread of man moreover took place in parallel with a biological development extending over rather more than three million years, and which started with small ape-like creatures capable of walking upright (*Australopithecines*), who lived in Africa and produced very simple stone tools; the creatures of the *Homo Habilis* type, who existed two million years ago, were slightly taller than the earlier *Australopithecines* and had a larger but still limited brain-volume. Then followed—in parallel with the Ice Age, whose drastic changes of climate brought about the extinction of many species—the first truly human types, who are collectively described as *Homo Erectus*. This genus, more than a million years old, which included the Heidelberg, Peking and Java people, had a brain of almost modern size and is known from the warmer parts of the whole ancient world. The most recent of the extinct human types, *Neanderthal Man*, which still existed 35,000 years ago, was only slightly different from the other types which several hundred thousand years ago replaced *Homo Erectus*. These types, including

	Spodsbjerg	Fosie	Voldtofte	Vejleby I	Vejleby II
Cattle	57%	(75%)	84%	47%	32%
Pigs	26%	(25%)	11%	26%	47%
Sheep	17%	(0%)	5%	28%	21%

Fig. 10. Percentage totals of the fragments of the major domesticated animals from various settlements at roughly one thousand year intervals in the southern part of Denmark/southernmost Scandinavia, respectively from the middle Neolithic period (Spodsbjerg, Langeland: early 3rd millennium BC), the late Bronze Age (Voldtofte (Kirkebjerget), south-western Fyn (Funen): early first millennium BC), the Roman Iron Age (Vejleby I, Lolland: early first millennium AD), and the end of the Viking Age/early Middle Ages (Vejleby II: early second millennium AD). Also included are the highly tentative observations (in round figures) from late Neolithic (early first millennium BC) Fosie, Skåne (Scania), a period from which, so far, no other settlement samples of animal bones have been analysed.

The interpretation of these percentages is difficult. Larger samples point first of all to environmental constraints on the composition of the stock of domestic animals, secondarily to the existence of other factors, such as distribution or trading of certain animals and meats, particular needs for textile production, etc. In the present case, the landscape around Vejleby seems to have become more forested with time (more pigs). The unusually high number of cattle-bones at Voldtofte may be related to the particularly high status of the site.

modern man, can all be grouped under the designation *Homo Sapiens*. The Neanderthals used fire, had relatively advanced stone tools and could adapt to life in the colder regions. Modern man developed a material culture which was very diversified and contained all the signs of the presence of abilities and perceptions equivalent to those of present man, although the culture of the late Ice Age was still that of the Stone Age hunter. This, our own type of man, migrated to Australia and America and was also responsible for the domestication of animals, the introduction of agriculture, the first villages and—from the fourth millennium BC onwards—the towns, and the whole of later development.

This knowledge, taken all in all, means that today we are relatively well-equipped to discuss the ecological conditions in pre-history, i.e. the relations between man and nature, or more accurately between physical and biological systems and man's ever more intensive manipulation of them. This manipulation has brought with it drastic changes in the relationship between open land and forest, often with soil erosion (after intensive farming), etc., as consequences (cf. fig. 9). But to imagine that in distant times there was no such thing as pollution or imbalance between exploitation of resources and their re-formation would not be in accord with present-day archaeological knowledge. Forests, for example, have been drastically reduced since the start of agriculture some 10,000 years ago and the connected exponential population growth.

To this should be added that general living conditions varied considerably, as is shown e.g. in the changing average height of genetically relatively stable populations. In Denmark, for instance, height in the male population rose steadily throughout the Stone Age, to stabilise at some point in the third millennium BC, remaining from then until the middle of the first millennium AD apparently at almost the same level as it is today. While the trends in the living conditions of women normally follow those for men, through the ages there can be seen a significant alteration in the number of severe injuries which can be observed in the skeleton material. In the Ice Stone Age, the Palaeolithic Age (the 'Old Stone Age'), the injuries were evenly divided between the two sexes, but in time they come to be found almost exclusively on the male skeletons. The men evidently had to bear the brunt of the heaviest physical work and were particularly exposed to serious accidents, violence and conflict. This is in no way to devalue the conditions of women, but it is clear that division of work between the sexes has had a very long history.

But living conditions should not be evaluated only on the basis of biological conditions. Mankind works and lives in what we call

ARCHAEOLOGY AND THE MAN-MADE MATERIAL REALITY

Fig. 11. The late Pre-Roman Iron Age settlement at Vorbasse, central Jutland, Denmark. The situation shortly before the birth of Christ shows two smaller farmsteads surrounded by irregular fences (cf. figs. 12-14).

nature, within organised structures, of which modern settlement archaeology has provided us with a number of particularly important representations—in Denmark, for example, from the hunter's small hut for the summer, on a stretch of water, the Stone Age farmer's square, post-built wooden house, to the Bronze

. ca. 1:3000.

0   50   100 m

Fig. 12. The late Roman Iron Age settlement at Vorbasse, central Jutland, Denmark. The situation in the fourth century shows a high number of larger farmsteads on their square fenced crofts (cf. figs. 11, 13, 14).

ARCHAEOLOGY AND THE MAN-MADE MATERIAL REALITY

Age and Iron Age long-house farm with the living quarters in one end, the stable at the other and two inner rows of roof-bearing posts. This last very characteristic form of building moreover lasted right up to the 12th century AD, and is thus an expression of a remarkable continuity in living- and working-structures within the area in question; Denmark and the adjacent areas lay far from the Mediterranean and the civilisations of antiquity and their many transitions and upheavals.

A good example of the results of modern settlement archaeo-logy, which often has international significance, is the village of Vorbasse in central Jutland (figs. 11-14). Here the settlement on the site started shortly before the birth of Christ with a few small Iron Age farms consisting of long houses surrounded by irregular palisade fences. In the third century AD the number of farmsteads grew considerably, and the now much larger long houses stood with various outhouses on large rectangular plots, private in nature, fenced in by palisades. This farm and village structure persisted until the eighth century, when the farm-plots again grew in size; on the plots stood very large, well-built long houses with curved long walls of Viking type, with diverse large outhouses along the fences. Around the year 1000 AD a dramatic change took place, in that the farmstead plots then took on a size of up to 120 x 200 metres, or 2½ hectares. In the middle of these plots stood the main building, a veritable hall. The animals were housed in separate sheds, which like the other out-houses, less elaborate dwelling-houses etc., were sited along the fences. Towards the end of the 12th century the village moved almost a kilometre, to the area around the medieval church in present-day Vorbasse, and there the village has remained until our own time.

It is very rare to be able to follow an entire settlement over such a long period, but a series of major excavations, particularly in Northern and North-western Europe, where excavation tech-niques are very advanced, have resulted in similar pictures. One of them is Feddersen Wierde, which dates from the first half of the first millennium AD and is situated on the North Sea coast west of the mouth of the Elbe. Here the preservation conditions for organic material are impressive, which means that e.g. the houses may be found preserved up to half the height of their

Fig. 13. The early Viking Age settlement at Vorbasse, central Jutland, Denmark. The situation around AD 800 shows a smaller number of big farmsteads in the enclosures (cf. figs. 11, 12, 14).

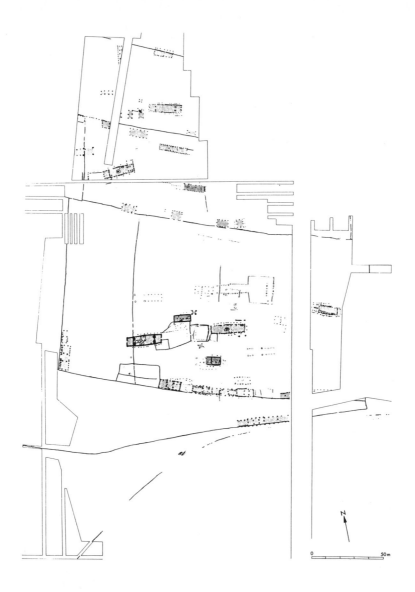

Fig. 14. The latest Viking Age settlement at Vorbasse, central Jutland, Denmark. The situation in the eleventh century AD shows a number of very big farmsteads, the largest in an enclosure of 120 by 200 metres (cf. figs. 11-13).

walls. Exceptionally good preservation conditions also account for a number of Stone and Bronze Age settlements in the area of the Alps. There is for instance a very large repertory of wooden implements from that area, and it has also been possible there to exploit to the full the dating technique of dendrochronology.

From a rather different world we can find another example in the compact mining village of Rocca San Silvestro, which is situated on a mountain top in Tuscany and which was abandoned in the 14th century AD; it too has been completely investigated (fig. 15). The walls, houses, church and defence-tower, etc. are built out of stone which has provided excellent preservation conditions. Here also highly skilled excavation has brought to light a huge quantity of material: artefacts, kitchen refuse, etc.; outside the village itself there have been investigations of a number of structures for extraction of metals which were delivered to the nearest main town, Pisa. There is no other place where one can gain such a complete impression of the material aspects of rural daily life in the Middle Ages. It is also very interesting that San Silvestro, in common with many other sites from the Middle Ages, displays distinct signs of wealth, much more so than e.g. corresponding Roman sites in the same region.

But the cultural landscape cannot be seen in its entirety until we move back from individual excavations and create a more-or-less complete overview of the settlement and all human activity in a larger local area or a whole region. Only then can we understand the sum of resources at the disposal of a group of hunters, or how an agrarian system worked with different settlements, fields, meadow-land, forests, etc., and how the individual settlement areas or villages related to each other, and what role they played within the larger social systems. In attempting to disentangle these relationships there are two possible approaches. Where the relationships permit, e.g. in the warmer areas such as the Mediterranean, with relatively shallow topsoil and many fragments of stone-built houses or hard-fired pottery which survive intensive ploughing and lengthy exposure on the surface, etc., one can undertake intensive surveys of traces of habitation in an area. Such surveys can also be used to outline long-term tendencies in the settlement

Fig. 15. The hill-top farming-mining settlement of Rocca San Silvestro, Campiglia, Tuscany (Italy). Abandoned in the early 14th century AD, it is a very rare case of a completely excavated medieval village with great potential for further economic and social analyses. Among other things, the complex yet simple technology involved is highly interesting, as well as the wealth of the individual households, which shows the medieval farmer to be far better off than his Roman predecessors. The written sources pertaining to the site are also plentiful.

and thus serve a geographical, a chronological and a historical purpose. In Northern Europe, for example, where a considerable depth of topsoil is often to be found, and building-customs in pre-history were almost exclusively based on wood, surveys are often less rewarding, apart from Stone Age sites with their rich flint material, which can frequently be identified on the surface. In these areas, therefore, more emphasis has to be placed on information which has already been collected from the relevant area, in Denmark for instance in the last 150 years or so, but supplementary surveys and studies of the soil conditions and the other characteristics of the landscape must also of course be carried out. To this must be added the always critical excavations of individual sites which can provide the necessary concrete and detailed information about the settlement (fig. 1).

A particular problem, which actually applies to all archaeology, but affects topographical conditions to a high degree, is bound up with the influence of the agriculture of later times on the find-picture (cf. fig. 23, and also figs. 24-25). On the one hand many finds are the result of agricultural activity, but on the other hand agriculture, extraction of raw materials, etc., even in past eras, have destroyed colossal quantities of information. For example, it is typical that the number of burial mounds, traces of field-systems from prehistory, etc. is much greater in old forests or in areas which have been forest until recently, than outside such areas. These circumstances are nowhere highlighted or discussed in detail, but important steps have now been taken to take these factors into account in the total research-picture, e.g. when archaeological surveys are made.

Naturally, it is still very difficult to cite areas where the older settlements and their resource potential are known virtually in their entirety. It is much easier to name regional investigations of individual phenomena, e.g. prehistoric field-systems or graves. Nevertheless a few examples exist of important general regional investigations of the above-mentioned kind. On the small island of Melos in the Aegean, for example, a number of modern surveys have been carried out of selected areas together with supplementary excavations, and at the same time a complete collection of earlier finds from all periods and of relevant written and historical data has been undertaken. This goes as far as anyone could hope. If the results even so seem rather thin, this is because the excavations here have been extremely limited in extent, and

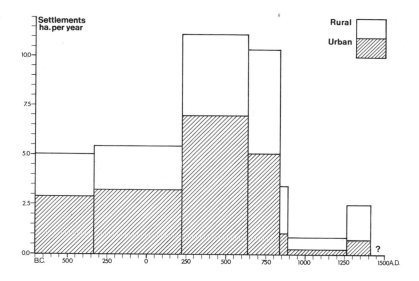

Fig. 16. The areas of rural and urban settlements respectively in an archaeologically very well-surveyed region of central Mesopotamia (Iraq). The settlement areas, reflecting changing numbers of population, economic activities etc., are calibrated for different lengths of periods. Note the collapse of settlement in the ninth century AD, under the ambitious Abbasid dynasty.

because the material in general is relatively meagre. Moreover, it is difficult to find optimal conditions for e.g. all periods or all phenomena in one and the same place or in one and the same region. The archaeological evidence must therefore normally be pieced together from many independent observations.

There are, however, very large quantities of material from both surveys and excavations which lend themselves particularly well to studies of diachronic—chronologically subdivided—spans, from the Near East, e.g. Mesopotamia (Iraq), where the history of the settlements in some selected areas can be closely determined over a period of more than five thousand years (fig. 16).

Middle Scandinavia, from south-west Norway to Gotland, has provided a number of fine examples of more-or-less contemporary farm constructions with their associated field-systems, out-field areas for grazing, graves, etc., often linked to pictures of a whole area and in several cases amplified by excavations, pollen analyses of the natural conditions, etc. The structures in most cases are from the second quarter of the first millennium AD, the late- and post-Roman period (or Migration period), when both the field boundaries and the walls of the farmhouses were built of stone and are therefore comparatively visible on the surface and relatively well-preserved (figs. 24-25).

The closest one can come to the ideal situation is perhaps the case of the extensive excavations carried out on the Altenhovener Platte west of Cologne in connection with open-cast lignite mining. There it was possible to identify virtually all significant traces of settlements, from the Stone Age to the Middle Ages and more recent times, over very large areas indeed. There have also been several comprehensive investigations along stretches of water, e.g. in southern Germany, which not only provided conditions which attracted Stone Age hunters and farmers, but have also created conditions for the preservation of organic materials, opportunities for pollen analyses, etc., which are near the optimal, giving information as to both local and regional situations.

And perhaps that is as close as we can expect to come. The populations of earlier times very seldom migrated to virgin land and even more seldom departed again from there with one accord. It is only to be expected that the archaeological landscape- and settlement-picture, at any rate in the beginning, will be hazy, and the structures in it difficult to distinguish. When we add to this the fact that one only has at one's disposal—as always in archaeology—fragments of a static sum-picture, from which the dynamic economic systems and societies of the past, in all their phases, are supposed to be reconstructed, the results already achieved actually begin to look impressive. It is particularly promising that settlement archaeology has already succeeded in wresting from the source material quantities of relevant and interesting data both on the man-made material reality as such and on the general history of an often very distant past.

5. Interpretations and Society

> So long as I rule over this kingdom
> we shall exchange treasures; friends shall greet
> one another with gifts from across the sea...
>
> The *Beowulf* Epic
> (end of the first millennium AD)

People live in continual interplay between the local community—the economy of everyday life and close social relations, reflected e.g. in settlement structures—and the larger world. Both in the everyday and in the larger context, they belong to a cultural community. The cultural community expresses itself materially in similarities—of house-types, burial customs, weapons, jewellery etc. But in order to understand the cultural context and in particular the changes within it, it is necessary to have a clear picture not only of the economic circumstances, but also of the family and social structure, together with the higher social organisation both within and beyond the local society and the individual region. It goes without saying that this is a difficult task, but it is not an impossible one, as we in fact recognize every single day in observing the material aspects of our own reality and explaining them by reference to other related circumstances, knowledge of our own history, norms, etc.

Some people might well claim that fundamentally every single element in our material culture is determined by our norms and in a manner of speaking becomes a signal of those norms. But if this alone controlled our view of the man-made material world we would have difficulty in dealing with the material in all its complexity. In a sense we would have returned to the earlier stage of research which I described in Chapter 3, in which the sum of a series of regionally-limited cutural features was considered an adequate definition of a 'culture', a social group, or even perhaps an ethnic or linguistic unit.

It would be just as wrong, however, not to look at the

functional and directly technological aspects of the find-material. A silver spoon with a round bowl and a short bar-shaped shaft is not just a thing which is characteristic of the beginning of the 17th century in European culture; it is also an object which can function as a spoon when a meal is being eaten. In addition it represents a piece of technology containing evidence of a long economic process which stretches from the silver-mine to the smithy, and which presupposes an engagement on the part of society at large in respect of organisation, transport, trade, etc. Moreover, a silver spoon has a special significance as a so-called investment-object and thus a social status-symbol, both within the family circle and in society in general. The spoon may indeed signal cultural norms, but it also does much more.

Now, however, the material reality consists not only of individual elements, no matter how informative they may be. The interpretations I have just presented in relation to the 17th century silver spoon are not built up merely on the basis of common sense, but also on real knowledge of the relevant period. This knowledge may have been acquired by reading documents or looking at pictures from that time, but we could also have constructed it—by the archaeological method—by studying the contexts in which different types of spoon have been found, e.g. damaged horn-spoons amongst other refuse in all households, whole silver spoons in hoards together with other valuable objects, perhaps marked with noble coats-of-arms. There are also other contexts, e.g. the find of a silversmith's workshop, etc., which can be important factors in understanding. Similarly, through the find-contexts, what is actually an archaeological information-base can gradually be built up around the other material aspects of the society and culture of the time, and its living conditions and norms.

In a typical archaeological situation, where as a rule it is only the finds with their information and the material objects that are available to us, it is important to have clearly in mind that the different types of find have to be treated in different ways where sociological and cultural interpretations of the material are concerned.

A refuse-pit is perhaps not a totally neutral reflection of the

ARCHAEOLOGY AND THE MAN-MADE MATERIAL REALITY

activities that have been carried on in the nearby house—the refuse would certainly have been sorted out with a view to possible re-use, and perhaps some categories of refuse were disposed of elsewhere, etc. But in any case in dealing with the material from a refuse-pit—in general in the course of settlement excavations—we can be reasonably sure that here we have a material which can, and should, be directly compared with other similar finds: the refuse from a castle, for example, with the corresponding debris from a farmyard, with the aim *inter alia* of analysing differences in living conditions and life-styles.

The case of finds which result from deliberate actions or rituals is different. Among these are e.g. finds of votive sacrifices and the very common grave-finds. The changing norms for burial, through the ages and in different areas, make it risky to compare such finds directly with each other in any respect other than the type of the grave. In some societies and contexts great emphasis was placed, for instance, on the provision of grave-goods, but in others this was not done. If one were uncritically to compare graves from an area with a 'rich' grave custom with those from a 'poor' one it would easily be possible to be led astray into drawing conclusions that would not necessarily be correct.

These two examples do not represent two situations which are totally different in essence, since all human actions of course have a cultural aspect; more precisely, they represent extreme points on a continuum. It can nevertheless be useful to keep them in mind, especially since many archaeologists all too often forget, in arguing their cases, the existence of contexts of these types. It is always important to be aware of the level at which one is operating in making observations, comparisons and drawing conclusions.

Often a break in continuity, for instance in burial customs, can be an important indicator that at this point one should be particularly careful about comparisons. In areas and periods with the same customs there is a certain basis for comparison, e.g. with a view to identifying richly-equipped graves as the graves of wealthy people. But even within a homogeneous framework there can be distinctions which have to be taken into account. On burial sites from the Iron Age on the Danish island of Bornholm, for example, it has been possible to show that the same prominent

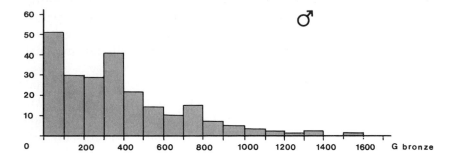

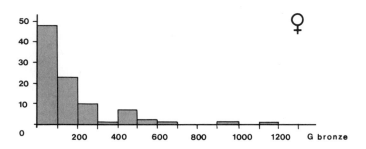

Fig. 17. The distribution of bronze invested in male and female burials respectively from the early Bronze Age period II (ending about 1300 BC) in Denmark. The investment in female graves is clearly at a lower level than in male ones. For both sexes, poorer graves are far more common than rich ones. Gold and artefacts conferring high status are found in the graves which are also rich in bronze. The latter are almost exclusively connected with men. (Cf. the illlustration on the cover and fig. 6).

family only marked out its status by the provision of rich grave-goods once in each generation.

Even if the graves are a difficult and risky find-group to deal with, it should not be forgotten that it is actually from them that we have obtained some of the most exciting information about the conditions of life in the past; one of the sources of this information is the skeleton material. Moreover, what the graves provide us with is a preserved picture of the single individual person, often with evidence as to clothing, ornaments, weapons, etc., although of course we cannot go on from there to interpret the picture to mean that this person appeared thus in everyday life. It is after all a ritual find, where we can expect anything from a 'naturalistic' presentation of the dead person and his/her role and status in society—a burial form which often seems to be associated with societies with a high degree of social mobility and competitiveness—to a very abstract and perhaps also meagre recording of some circumstance or other which is often impenetrable to us.

A large investigation of the quantities of metal invested in the several thousand burial-mound graves in Denmark from the early Bronze Age, the latter half of the second millennium BC, has drawn attention to a number of interesting facts (fig. 17; cf. the illustration on the cover, and fig. 6). The investment in bronze was considerably greater in the male graves than in the female graves, and there were many more poorly-equipped graves than richly-equipped ones in both groups. In the graves rich in bronze, moreover, there was found by far the largest proportion of the gold, typically associated with men. In the rich male graves, e.g. with swords, and virtually only there, there were also found a number of objects, however, whose production did not require large quantities of bronze, and which in theory could just as well have been found in the poor graves, but which were not found there. These included wooden folding chairs with bronze nails or mountings, small ornamental plaques with a raised centre (but not the equivalent type with a point, which is found in both rich and poor graves and both male and female ones), staves with end-mounts of bronze, certain types of tools, etc.

These 'cheap' bronze objects were thus specially linked to the richly-equipped male graves, containing objects which were even made of imported materials, since bronze and gold were not to be found naturally in the country. As folding chairs, staves, particular ornaments etc. should evidently be perceived as signs of status—no doubt with a 'political' content—here we have an interesting linkage of social roles, social status and a major investment in expensive grave-goods of exotic raw-materials. In this example we thus have grounds to assume that grave-wealth can be 'translated' into general wealth where the individual, his family and their social setting are concerned.

For many of these Bronze Age graves, it is also true that their orientation seems to be determined by the time of year in which the buried person died. The normal practice is that the dead person 'faces towards' the dawn on the day of the burial; in one particular region, however, it is sunset to which the body's face is turned, but the principle is the same. This observation shows that in the Bronze Age burial was not just a marking of social relations, using the language of the norms of southern Scandinavia, but that life's last crisis was connected to the whole world picture. This is not unexpected, but it can rarely be demonstrated with a convincing degree of probability—and here only on the basis of remains of plants in the graves which can demonstrate the time of the year, and differences in the winter and summer garments. At the major contemporary ritual structure at Stonehenge in southern England—with its main axis aligned with significant celestial points where the sun would be found at certain times—it has long ago proved possible to show the existence of relations of this type in the Bronze Age.

As can be seen from these examples, it is primarily through contextual investigations that it has apparently been possible to break the cultural codes and translate them into relations that are recognisable to us. If we had not been able to do this we would have been limited to merely describing the archaeological phenomena.

I should like to introduce one further example of how this type of approach to the work can lead to understanding of the social and ideological conditions in the past; here, however, the find material is more varied than in the foregoing. In the previous chapters we considered in detail the development of the Danish village of Vorbasse, in central Jutland (figs. 11-14). In the third century AD a distinct rearrangement of the settlement there took place, and thereafter it consisted of large farmsteads (predominantly longhouses) on enclosed plots all of about the same size and of a 'private' character. This rearrangement can best be interpreted as a stabilisation of the family structure and especially of the family's rights—perhaps acquired through generations— to e.g. the means of production, linked with a stronger superior social organisation, which resulted in a module-like partitioning of the land and the farm-plots.

Such a view can be supported by the evidence of other finds and find-categories, in that the third century AD is also in a number of other respects a time of change. In the graves the grave-goods, which included, among other things, a number of Roman luxury objects, were considerably reduced, which can be interpreted as an expression of a lower degree of social mobility and individual competition; it was definitely not the case that society became poorer. But at the same time many more women than previously were given a burial of a certain distinction. This could indicate that the position of women was improving, e.g. in association with a stable family structure with clearer inheritance patterns.

Among the ritual finds from the bogs can be seen a distinct group which comprises sacrifices of warrior-equipment, seemingly from defeated armies. These armies would be military units of several hundred men, foot-soldiers and horsemen, equipped with Roman swords etc., but otherwise with weaponry of a Germanic character. These finds disclose, on the one hand, that a military organisation and without doubt a command or leadership existed, and also, on the other, that the changes in society of which the Vorbasse village provides evidence were accompanied by problems and conflicts. Potential conflicts no doubt were also expressed in the contemporary long ramparts which divided off various regions from others. Last, but not least, it should be mentioned that at this time there also arose large and very wealthy chieftain- or royal centres (with farmsteads, workshops, religious areas, etc.) such as Gudme on Funen, in Denmark (fig. 18). This settlement, which occupied at least a couple of hundred hectares, lies only four kilometres from a coastal settlement, more than half a kilometre long, at Lundeborg, which must have been controlled by the Gudme centre. At the Lundeborg site there are traces of many different craft activities and of trade, probably of a seasonal nature. Several ships of this period have been found in Denmark.

It would not have been unnatural to have included examples from the classical civilisations or other societies where the contextual

Fig. 18 (facing page). The Gudme-Lundeborg area, south-eastern Fyn (Funen), Denmark. Key localities and finds. Contours at ten metre intervals; areas surrounded by dotted lines are bogs and meadows.

The area holds a very rich royal centre, late Roman Iron Age-Migration period, with a coastal emporium. The lay-out of the area, its organisation and maintenance, were far from grandiose, however; the character of the individual settlements was rather that of enlarged villages with craft activity and trading areas. A number of religious localities are inferred from the place-names and from artefacts, but their form is unknown.

Symbols: Open triangle = pre-Roman and Roman Iron Age cemetery of Møllegårdsmarken; black triangle = settlement contemporary with Møllegårdsmarken cemetery; A = Late Roman and Migration Period emporium (harbour and crafts settlement) at Lundeborg; B = major concentrantions at Gudme of metal finds from the period AD 200 to 1000 (mainly of the fifth century) in the top-soil (revealed by metal detector); C = excavated Late Roman-Migration period farmsteads; dots = major hoards from the Migration period; crosses = High Medieval parish churches.

working method can be supported e.g. by information from written sources. On the other hand it is important to emphasise the inherent power of the material sources, particularly with regard to relations over and above the purely technical and economic. The one area which I feel should also be mentioned here is the aesthetic, which plays such a large role in e.g. classical and near-Eastern archaeology (cf. fig. 19). Buildings, monuments and products such as temples, statues, decorated vases and even wooden buildings—e.g. the halls of the Viking Age—paleolithic cave-paintings, decorated Neolithic pottery and metal objects from the Bronze Age can moreover easily be related to the social and economic conditions which have played an important role in this chapter.

Aesthetic efforts have apparently always been appreciated, and the aesthetic aspect has been used as a central element in social interplay, both in the form of general cultural codes and as a means of promoting a particular individual or a particular group—in socially stratified societies, of course, especially in the

ARCHAEOLOGY AND THE MAN-MADE MATERIAL REALITY

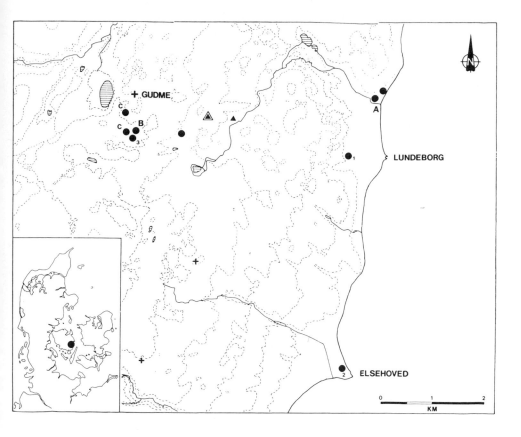

case of expensive products. For instance, the so-called zoomorphic ornamentation—an abstract and emblematic minimal art for ornamental use—constituted a general code characterising the Germanic warrior élite around whom the myths grew up which are related, for example, in the Beowulf poem, from which a quotation has been taken above. This international warrior class actually arose precisely at the same time as the changes in society discussed above in relation to the Vorbasse village (cf. fig. 2). The traditional artistic naturalism of the Greek and Greek-influenced societies of classical antiquity, and of e.g. the Roman Empire, in spite of quantities of Roman glass, bronze vessels, swords, silver coins etc., which all witness to close connections between the societies in question, found no echo on this side of the Roman Rhine-Danube border. The objects referred to could be incorporated into a Germanic society with an interest in luxury versions of functionally familiar objects, while naturalistic art was closely linked to the classical city-state and the later empires, whose furthest border in the north was the Roman *limes*. Ironically enough naturalism in the Roman Empire was weakened in exactly the same late period, and there, too, ornamental art became for a time the prevailing idiom as the discreet symbol of power.

As the discussion and examples in this chapter have shown, it seems that all things—material and other—hang together; apparently all that is unknown is nevertheless susceptible to handling and open to understanding. Even the polarities are apparently connected through the ideological traditions and cultural norms which cut across society and economic processes in the long course of history.

Fig. 19 (facing page). City-planning in the late Classical and Hellenistic periods at Olynth, northern Greece, fourth century BC. Multiple functions, the clear separation of these, monumental construction, and conspicuous architectural landscapes, even the creation of artificial landscapes, are typical of the late city-states at the time of the rise of the Hellenistic empires, of which the Roman Empire is the crowning achievement.

ARCHAEOLOGY AND THE MAN-MADE MATERIAL REALITY

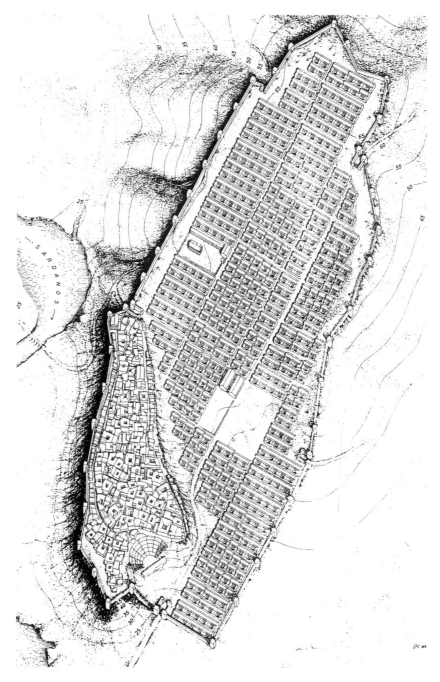

6. Archaeology and History

This is the race of iron. Now, by day,
Men work and grieve unceasingly; by night,
They waste away and die. ...
Hesiod (c. 700 BC)

Written sources often reflect a particular opinion—as does this book—and they must therefore be treated with caution when it comes to drawing conclusions from them. For times as distant as antiquity, the written material is moreover written by a small number of people near the top of society and it deals primarily with political, religious and literary subjects—often with a decided slant. In a situation such as this the archaeological source material therefore has a particularly great significance, in that it is independent of social élites, even if it naturally also includes those élites and their activities.

In modern societies we have great respect for the written word, and it is also to the written sources that history primarily has recourse. With the steady growth of material sources, however, a new situation is arising, in which archaeology is beginning to write history, or to seek a historical dimension, primarily in areas such as the general development of society, the economy, cultural norms, etc. This of course means that our traditional pictures concerning a number of points have to be extended and altered; but it also means that the world is growing larger.

Methodologically, however, we do not face greater difficulties than those I have already touched on in the preceding chapters. The professional means which the history-seeking archaeologist has primarily to bring into use will be ecology, the subsistence-economy, settlement-research, the supra-regional economy, including trade and exchange, and the studies of local, regional and international social structures and cultural norms—all of them subjects whose character we have dealt with above. Archaeology's historical potential lies in the general character of the material, its universal diffusion in relation to place and time and its possibilities for illuminating phenomena over long chronological sequences, for instance settlement-development in a region. Archaeology has developed a good apparatus for description and dating, but still experiences difficulties, relatively speaking, in the explanation of many phenomena. That said, however, the situation is not different from that in cultural, social and historical disciplines in general, even if the work has to adapt to the broader time-span with which the profession—despite C-14 dating and dendrochronology—normally has to work.

Archaeology, apart from local history, is perhaps particularly suited to throw light on the 'large' historical questions such as the basic changes in political, economic and social systems. A good example of this is the fall or transformation of the Roman Empire, which as is familiar from written history comprised the western Roman Empire's political and military collapse in 476 AD and the reduced eastern Roman Empire's continuation in the Byzantine Empire, coming to a close only with the Turkish conquest of Constantinople (Istanbul) in the summer of 1453 (cf. fig. 22).

The primary modern archaeological contribution to the history of the Roman Empire is the analysis of the settlement system, in both town and country, together with the supply or subsistence economy which completely dominated the societies of antiquity, of whatever type. To this can be added areas such as general economy, the military system and investment in monuments, of which e.g. classical archaeology has provided innumerable excavations and descriptions. The settlement studies reveal *inter alia* a dramatic increase in the number of villas and farms in the areas near Rome in the centuries around the birth of Christ, when the city was the undisputed centre of the Empire. Such an extreme increase of population (for reasons of supply and work) in and around the large centre is known also from other ancient civilisations and must have been a constant burden on the societies, even if the phenomenon seldom lasted more than a few hundred years at a time. Rome was also threatened by another development, though a less dramatic one, which later took place in the western provinces, where settlement peaked around 200 AD. After that there was a constant decline of both towns and country in the north-western part of the Roman Empire, whose 'fall' in 476 AD was thus the result of processes which had started more than 500 years earlier. In spite of the military conflicts, on which the chronicle-writers naturally enough focus their attention, the fall of the western Roman Empire was more accurately the result of an undermining of the subsistence economy and the market system. It is also probably no coincidence that the Germanic societies which in late Roman times challenged the Roman west themselves went through a radical change precisely in the third century AD—as mentioned several times in the preceding chapter.

In contrast, in the Levant, one of the most prominent parts of the eastern Roman Empire, the period around 500 AD, when the west was politically and militarily written off, was experienced as a veritable boom, both in terms of settlements and as regards the agricultural economy. Not until the later wars of attrition with the Persian Empire over the control of the Middle East did this development begin to turn into recession—perhaps primarily because of problems in its political economy—and the way was prepared for the surprising Islamic conquest of the mid 7th century.

This representation can be supplemented by archaeological and historical studies of transport conditions and of trade in foodstuffs, pottery and other products, by reference to the frequency of building of early Roman public buildings, late Roman and Byzantine churches, etc., and by much else. From area to area and from period to period throughout the Roman Empire, the Mediterranean region and the Middle East, however, we can see an identical and now familiar picture, the main element of which is the significant connection between population-developments, the subsistence economy and political history (fig. 22).

In this way archaeology has been able to provide the contours of an explanation of this very important passage in history.

The interplay between writing and things can also be demonstrated in another example, taken from the Viking Age, the end of the first millennium AD in Northern Europe. In the marketplace or emporium of Birka, in central Sweden, near Stockholm, a number of graves with Islamic coins have been found. The coins are an insignificant proportion of the hundreds of thousands of silver *dirhems* which at that time flowed from the Middle East into

ARCHAEOLOGY AND THE MAN-MADE MATERIAL REALITY

Fig. 20. Detail of pictorial carvings on the inner side of the stones of a grave-cist from a very large cairn at Kivik in eastern Skåne (Scania), present-day Sweden. Ca. 1300 BC. The two-wheeled horse-drawn chariot is an international type of vehicle, known among the Bronze Age élites as far afield as central Scandinavia and the Near East. Several (real) chariots of this type were included in the famous tomb of Pharao Tut-ank-Amun, who died in ca. 1350 BC.

67

Russia and Scandinavia. The first wave, which arrived about 800 AD, had been coined in Mesopotamia—some of them in Baghdad, the capital of the Caliphate—and the next and apparently larger wave came from Turkestan, partly from the fabled Samarkand, in the years around 900 AD. This pattern closely reflects the development within the Islamic realm, including the collapse of Mesopotamia around the middle of the ninth century (which the settlement studies in general also reflect (cf. fig. 16)) and the subsequent rise of the provinces.

The import of Islamic silver was of decisive significance for the Nordic region and perhaps primarily for the development of southern Scandinavia, which around 800 AD was threatened by the expanding Carolingian Empire which dominated the continent. The cessation of the flow of silver must have been extremely aggravating to e.g. the Danish élite, who in fact initiated a series of plunder-campaigns in western Europe in precisely the years between the two influxes of silver. These raids ceased almost from one year to the next when the new Islamic silver arrived around 900 AD. The reduction in the flow of silver in the ninth century actually runs parallel to a general contour of instability, in which Christian Europe suffered attacks not only from the Nordic Vikings, but also from migrant Hungarians and—in the Mediterranean—Moslems. The Carolingian Empire's decline also meant, however, that the regional resources in western Europe developed, and the stable village settlements, markets and growing numbers of towns characteristic of the time after 1000 AD became a reality.

Again in this example, from the late first millennium AD, archaeology has been able to provide decisive information and render comprehensible the processes which characterised the historical development. It will therefore now be an exciting challenge to try to use studies such as those mentioned as models for the description, both mega-historical and more detailed, regional or even local, of the conditions in the periods and areas where the written source-material is distinctly meagre or does not exist at all.

Or, in other words, to stretch the span of social history back into the pre-Christian millennia.

ARCHAEOLOGY AND THE MAN-MADE MATERIAL REALITY

This is a very difficult task, but also one which is full of promise, and which can take its departure-point in the large stock of traditional knowledge which already exists, for instance concerning find-objects and phenomena which occur in several different areas and can therefore indicate possible contacts between societies, along with the nature of those contacts. But the main thrust of the work ought to follow approximately the work-process I have outlined several times above: analyses of natural resources, subsistence economy, settlement, the larger economic and social system and the cultural and ideological traditions.

On the mega-historic level we have to reckon, in the pre-Christian millennia, with fewer direct links across great distances between societies than in the first, and still less the second, millennia AD. But this does not mean that e.g. the European societies and cultures—despite their differences—were not already then part of a community.

The existence of such a community can probably be traced right back to the hunting Stone Age, with synchronic changes in types of tools, e.g. arrow-heads, over very large distances—so large that they cannot be explained by the seasonal migrations of the hunting tribes. With the Neolithic or farming Stone Age societies became stationary, but on the other hand there began a comprehensive exchange of raw materials and of products, even though the essential products—then as in later millennia—continued to be produced within the local area. An example of the exchange of raw materials is the so-called trade in obsidian, from the Middle East and elsewhere, which was discussed in Chapter 3 above (fig. 7). An exchange of ideas, knowledge and experience concerning natural conditions and production techniques—probably centering on common problems—also took place in the later part of the farming Stone Age, when the ox-drawn plough and cart were introduced into large areas of Europe at about the same time, just before and around 3000 BC, along with the exploitation of the products farm animals can supply while they are alive: milk, wool—and of course tractive power.

In central Europe around 3000 BC, there was also the an increasing production of copper (and gold), which was used for products which came to play a large role for Stone Age societies,

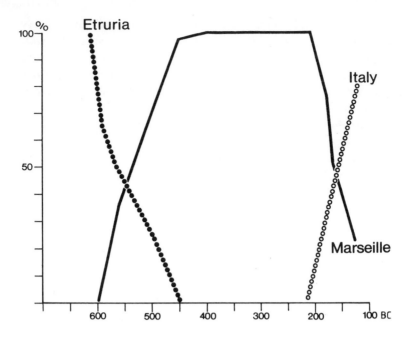

Fig. 21. The changing places of origin of the foreign ceramics from the period about 600 to about 100 BC found on settlement-sites in the south-eastern part of France outside the town of Marseille. So-called amphorae for the transportation of foodstuffs account almost exclusively for the percentages of sherds in the diagram.

partly because of the highly valued status they conferred, and probably from then onwards they were among the preconditions for the development of the social élites which characterised the Bronze Age in the second millennium BC. At any rate, these élites were responsible for the emergence of close contacts, even if still mostly indirect in nature, between the different parts of Europe. These contacts resulted in e.g. weaponry of the same type, such as swords and spears, and advanced vehicles in the form of light two-wheeled horse-drawn chariots (fig. 20).

ARCHAEOLOGY AND THE MAN-MADE MATERIAL REALITY

Another important line of development began in Mesopotamia around the middle of the fourth millennium BC—and slightly later in Egypt—with the appearance of city-states and administrative élites, as a rule linked to temples. In third-millennium western Eurasia, there could therefore be found both contacts over large areas and significant differences between e.g. the Near-Eastern and Continental European societies. This gap was further accentuated when the palace-centred economies began to appear in Greece—in Crete around 2000 BC, on the mainland a little later. The Greek palace society and most similar structures in the Near East collapsed at the end of the second millennium BC, at the transition to the Iron Age. It was only in Egypt and Mesopotamia that the civilisations survived this decisive crisis and transformation.

In Greece around the end of the second millennium BC we can observe how a form of society which had parallels in the European hinterland had developed as an alternative to the palace cultures. In the centuries around and after 1000 BC certain characteristic features emerged which were common to almost all of Europe; these features were related to the 'Homeric' ideology adopted by the elites of those societies, with their preoccupation with the martial virtues and hospitality—as is revealed in the finds of armoury, weapons and drinking vessels. For instance, the same type of bronze pail (for drinks) was to be found in use at that time from central Italy to Denmark.

But the emergence of the classical Greek city-states and their commercial economy set up new divisions between the societies of Europe, and created a series of centre-periphery relations which for some societies resulted in dependence and for others in exclusion (cf. fig. 21). The creation of empires in the Mediterranean and Middle East in the latter half of the first millennium BC did not affect this process, even though the expansion of the Roman Empire brought the Mediterranean organisation far into temperate Europe, and thus made even the distant Nordic region directly dependent on events far, far away to the south.

These examples and perspectives, mainly concerned with the mega-historical use of archaeological material, have been taken from far-distant times. It almost goes without saying that the methods and work-processes could just as easily have been applied to much later times than those dealt with here—even to the present, where studies linking material aspects of local and supra-regional life and society are still regrettably rare.

The history of material reality is total.

Nevertheless, the material does not make up the only or the entire reality.

Where the past is concerned, the 'picture' (or the 'style'), and in particular what is 'written down', have often had special significance attributed to them. The reality of the style or picture (a crystallization of the meeting of the thought and the individual with tradition) is, however, predominantly bound to the material. The reality of what is written, of the document or the book, cannot however be so easily pinned down. The methodological difficulties in trying to unite the material and the written media are obviously very great. In spite of this the attempt must be made, and in actual fact archaeologists are thoroughly experienced in this, even though they seldom reflect on it. A large part of archaeological work consists of reading and evaluating what other archaeologists have written, and of creating new syntheses from it.

The route that has to be steered towards a combination of the material and the written seldom therefore follows a direct line between the two media, but has to be found by creating a third which can unite the two, and eventually also other, media. This third medium is the historical and social-historical scenario or model in its ever-changing form—flowing as it does, with the current of cognition in the sea of research personalities.

By constantly presenting a revised historical picture it is therefore relatively easy to test against it both materials and assertions—and thus, very often, to create new and altered scenarios. By this means the disparities between different types of data are resolved, and we can devote ourselves to understanding, rather than to methodological sophistry or, when things go really badly, the battle between academic disciplines or their traditions and their different types of material.

The mega-historical reality is therefore both finite and ever-changing; philosophically it is finite, but academically it is infinite.

ARCHAEOLOGY AND THE MAN-MADE MATERIAL REALITY

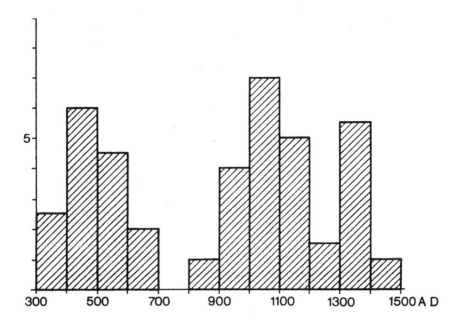

Fig. 22. Changing frequencies of church-building (or major alterations) in Constantinople—capital city of the eastern Roman and Byzantine empires—up to the end of the Christian metropolis in AD 1453.

The decline of even the eastern Roman Empire is noted in the drastically reduced building activity in the city during the seventh and the eighth centuries AD. Also visible is the so-called middle Byzantine recovery, the new decline after the occupation of the crusaders, and the final cultural expansion of the Byzantine renaissance which did not, however, outlive the Turkish conquest. The graph, however prosaic at first glance, is a powerful reminder of the interrelations of ideological, political, economic and cultural factors and of the use of archaeology in the estimation of the material character of historical developments.

7. Archaeological Institutions

> ... do not let your life
> be governed by what discomforts you.
> Abu al-Ala al-Ma'arri (973-1057)

The institutional framework of archaeology in its early days was relatively simple, since it consisted virtually exclusively of private collections and *Kunstkammers*, as a rule belonging to princes, who collected curiosities or decorated their homes with classical sculptures. There were significant changes in the last century, when archaeology became public, linked to what were then rather small museums, primarily in the capitals and larger towns (cf. fig. 3). It was from these organisations that much, and often most, of the basic work originated. It was also there that the archaeological source material and other data which form the basis for research were conserved, preserved and registered.

In the second half of the 18th century interest in Antiquity took on a special form, in that bourgeois forces opposing the late-feudal society sought models in classical Antiquity for new forms of behaviour and society. This is evident from the role which the study of classical art acquired—a role which can be seen not only in the budding academic writing, but also in the contemporary art and literature. After the Napoleonic Wars, in the new bourgeois society, the study of Antiquity had already been 'tamed' and slid gently, just like the study of the historic periods, into the academic frame of reference of the 19th century. This frame of reference, as is known, was characterised by an academic perspective in which description of data and documentation of knowledge were central, and in which the dissemination of this knowledge—at any rate to the social élite—was treated as essential.

In the universities, classical archaeology was expanded in the course of the 19th century, in close association with philology, art history and other classical studies, while the so-called prehistoric, or rather general, archaeology was often considered to be insufficiently academic to be taken up in the honourable company of philosophers, philologists, historians, etc. In certain cases general archaeological activities also took place, however, in association with the natural science faculties in the universities. But not until later did the demand arise for a truly general archaeological education—in Denmark, for instance, only around the time of the Second World War.

In this century classical archaeology has by and large remained firm in its academic affiliations to the other classical subjects and to art history, while the prehistoric—or general—research tradition has had more complex affiliations, depending e.g. on what country is in question. In Northern Europe, for example, the basic ties have been humanistic, in the U.S.A. pronouncedly sociological ('anthropology' there covers ordinary archaeology, social anthropology and physical, i.e. biological, anthropology), while there are also examples, e.g. from the Netherlands, of prehistoric or general archaeology having strong links with the natural sciences. Near Eastern archaeology has followed a path similar to that of classical archaeology and is also often connected with it, but it is characteristic of both these traditions, especially in recent times, linked as they are first and foremost to the study of the ancient civilizations—and thereby to the élitist Near-Eastern/European cultural heritage—that they have taken new inspiration from prehistoric archaeology with its general archaeological methods, work-processes and perspectives—or 'approaches'. The same applies to another new growth on the stem, which was not linked to the universities until recently, i.e. the archaeology of the Middle Ages and more recent times. Medieval archaeology is also strongly influenced—indeed sometimes almost intimidated—by traditional history, which recently, however, has also become preoccupied with material sources as a valuable supplement to an old discipline. It is still all too rare to find historians recognising the autonomy of the material sources and their particular potential.

On the surface these relationships may perhaps seem peripheral to the development of archaeology and research, but that is far from the case. Disciplines which deal with human beings are a battle for human souls, precisely in the same way as are our own views of the world. Moreover, the framework dictates the form

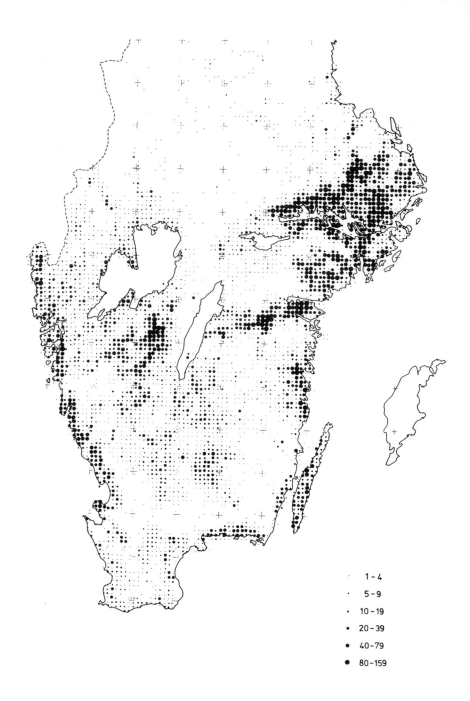

·	1 – 4
·	5 – 9
·	10 – 19
●	20 – 39
●	40 – 79
●	80 – 159

ARCHAEOLOGY AND THE MAN-MADE MATERIAL REALITY

Fig. 23 (facing page). Distribution of prehistoric cemeteries, largely of Iron Age date, in present-day southern Sweden (the island of Gotland excluded). As expected, for population and subsistence reasons, the sites are concentrated in the major agricultural regions. There are few such cemeteries, however, in the fertile area of Skåne (Scania) in the southern-most part of Sweden (the former Danish areas), which was no doubt also heavily populated in the Iron Age, but where open land cemeteries were probably largely destroyed by the later, very intensive land-use. This map is a result of modern computer-aided central administrative archaeo-logical recording.

taken by research, teaching and other work, and to a high degree determines both what priorities one has and what is seen as good academic work, and can thus ensure the practitioner the social ascent which perhaps the norms of modern society in particular presuppose.

In the realm of museums the first half of this century saw a constant expansion, and in several countries—e.g. Denmark—it was still in that context that archaeological research primarily took place. After the Second World War, and especially in the 1960s, the museums received very large sums of public money, which were however the result of legal provisions which imposed clear requirements on the institutions in the primary museological area, *inter alia* in terms of setting up displays rather than pursuing the research which was being carried out.

In the first place this meant less. Archaeology, especially the prehistoric or general archaeology, expanded considerably in the light of the increased national resources. At the same time the universities entered, as we know, a phase of explosive growth which was also beneficial to research, and particularly experimental research. The problems for archaeological research did not reveal themselves until the growth in funding could no longer continue, and a series of structural and other problems pushed their way to the forefront in the period leading up to the 1990s.

But before we evaluate this situation, we should examine yet another very important element in the development, i.e. the legal

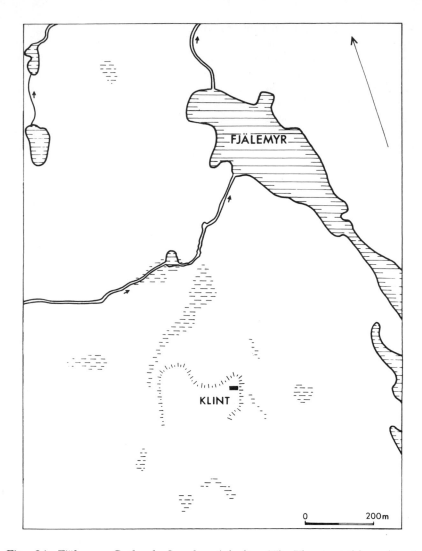

Fig. 24. Fjäle on Gotland, Sweden (cf. fig. 25). The invisible cultural landscape before detailed studies in the area. According to the register of ancient monuments, there was only a house foundation (the black rectangle) from the early Iron Age, suggesting a small farmstead deserted in the sixth century AD.

Fig. 25 (facing page). Fjäle on Gotland, Sweden (cf. fig. 24). The 'invisible' cultural landscape after a careful study of the area. We note a highly complex and well-preserved agricultural landscape comprising

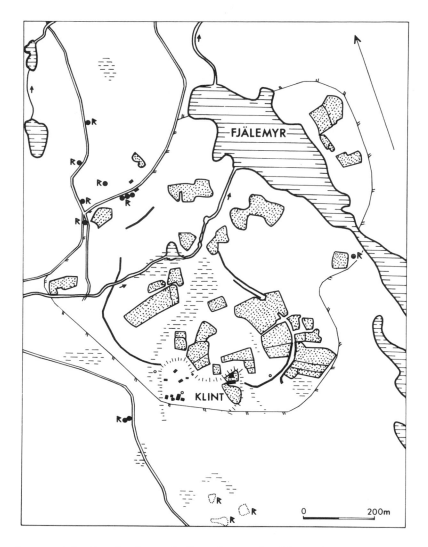

farms originating in the early Iron Age and with continuous occupation till the mid-fourteenth century AD.

Symbols: Black square (etc.) = building; Runic R = single grave; Runic R within broken line = cemetery; circle = well; bold line = stone wall; serrated line = wooden fence; double line = road; dashes = wetlands; area of dashes and parallel lines within unbroken line = bog or marshland; dotted area within unbroken line = fields.

provisions and practice associated with the 'cultural heritage'—as it is known, in a virtually ineradicable and rather monstrous expression (cf. fig. 1). In fact the monuments in the landscape attracted attention at an early stage and particularly in the last century they acquired the nature of important symbols of the nation-state. It can also be mentioned that, characteristically, the 'Riksantikvarieämbetet' (Office of the State Antiquary) in Sweden was actually established in the 'Imperial Period' in the 17th century, when—almost in Roman style—there was a physical and spiritual mobilisation of society for the maintenance of Sweden's domination over her empire.

The first efforts in the field of preservation of historical monuments in recent times in large parts of Europe consisted of ensuring the protection of at least some of the visible monuments: from Roman ruins, megalithic graves and burial mounds to castles and churches. But after the Second World War, when settlement archaeology demonstrated the enormous cultural-historical potential which can exist invisibly under open fields, an understanding emerged in the processes of law for the value of remains of this type as well (cf. fig. 23 and figs. 24-25). This has resulted, today, especially in Western European countries, in large-scale archaeo-logical activity being conducted in connection with building-work, motorway construction, the laying of gas pipelines, etc. At the same time there has been a significant improvement in the re-gistration of historical monuments in relation to this work, which combines general protection efforts with investigations originating out of modern society's often heavily destructive demands.

Today very significant resources are placed at the disposal of archaeological administration, preservation and conservation measures, exhibitions, archives, etc.—resources to which the previous generation of archaeologists could hardly have dreamt of having access. All these operations are carried out, of course, in a scientific way, and many investigations, e.g. of settlements, conducted in association with major construction works—for in-stance, the Altenhovener Platte investigations (chapter 4)—are of very great significance in the research context. This is also true of the large-scale data-recording projects which are being carried out e.g. by the Danish National Museum, which has one of the world's largest and oldest topographical archives of finds and prehistoric monuments. Mention should also be made of the many new and often impressive and cleverly-composed exhibitions which are presented these days, many of them as temporary special exhibitions, others as permanent and as a rule 'public-friendly' displays. Through these exhibitions—to a much greater extent than through publications—the 'dialogue' with the law-makers and the state and other authorities about resources is carried on.

In the light of this massive effort there has been a total change in archaeological practice—i.e. what in fact is undertaken. From being a small academic discipline with a strong museum component and as a rule a relatively weak basis in the universities, archaeology has developed to be an expanding field with large sections for cultural administration, many large and small museums, university institutes, etc. This ensures that a number of tasks which are important for research can be carried out, but it does not guarantee that basic research will receive the same encouragement as other activities. In the museums the research function has evidently been weakened, and the universities have clearly entered into a critical readjustment process.

For the public the ideal nationally administered archaeological system seems today to consist of a cultural-monument administration which administers protection and the legally-required investigations, museums which keep the finds and the collected information along with—not least—putting on exhibitions, and finally universities which educate the next generation of archaeologists.

In circumstances such as these, in a game such as this, the fact is that basic research, and thus the academic tradition of archaeology, are at risk. We have built up a system which administers and organizes a source material and a field of learning which as a matter of fact is not static, but which nevertheless does not develop anything like as fast as the source-material increases—or even one might say as fast as the rest of society changes. We have in other words reached what is virtually a 'post academic' stage, in which legal provisions and administration have created a practice which cannot be said to be of service to basic research, and which therefore is not conducive to the creation of new knowledge and new understanding.

From being a method of coming to understand part of the world, archaeology is on the way to becoming a static idiom—a symbol. But of what?

8. Conclusion

> The course of an arrow and that of the soul
> are different.
>
> Marcus Aurelius (121-180 AD).

It is not difficult to round off this book. I have said what I wanted to say; to repeat it, even to summarise, would therefore be superfluous and would only increase the uncertainty, and particularly the uneasiness, one feels when one has shared with others reflections which are in some ways very personal, even if they concern professional subjects.

As a student, when in spite of many other opportunities I chose to stay in archaeology—and the choice was not difficult—it was above all the adventure, the possibility of accomplishing and experiencing something new, which made me refrain from going on to some other field. The professional milieu also demonstrated to me the necessity for precision and documentation—the methodology of academic positivism. But the true driving forces were something I fortunately had to find for myself, often from outside archaeology. In time I also began, occasionally, to create them myself.

Nevertheless, the future is something I am reluctant to express views on. One can always sketch out plans, but one scarcely knows in what direction one will go oneself. One can evaluate the present and express opinions, but that does not make the future more definite, and certainly not for others, who have themselves to choose their place in archaeology and in archaeological research.

As human beings we are so fundamentally different from each other that it would not be appropriate to try to say something supposedly definite about which direction archaeological practice, and still less basic research, will or should take. I am convinced, however—and this can be taken as an article of faith—that there

ARCHAEOLOGY AND THE MAN-MADE MATERIAL REALITY

will be a process of interaction with all the other things that will happen in the academic world and especially in the rest of society, and that this process will determine e.g. what subjects we take up and in what way. There exists a close interplay between the history of archaeology and that of society. An archaeologist can therefore not get far without inspiration from his own society. On the slightly more philosophical level this intimacy also extends to the source material which—although created in the past—only exists in the present, which is the only time we know, and which is our only starting point.

In Venice, where the nights are made for strolling, and where pleasure is as clear and actual as the eye which glides casually across decaying history, one can contemplate the trophies of antiquity looted by the crusaders. As heralds from a distant reality they belong both to the Middle Ages and to our own time (fig. 26). And from there we can let our vision and thoughts travel to the monuments which much later took Venice as their model, perhaps even these very details, and made them actual (fig. 27). Each age thus has its own autonomy, each society, each individual, its experiences and its specific character, even if our biology, behaviour, learning, experience and economic, social and cultural behaviour also link us together and have produced a number of structural convergences in the long course of history.

All the same, one can only think and—where the material remains are concerned—see back into the past through one's own present, one's own hastily accumulated reality. I have thus here been able to deal only with archaeology's experience until the present—as it

Fig. 26. Highly decorated column and capitals from the church of Saint Polyeuktos in Constantinople (Sarachane, Istanbul) in front of the church of San Marco in Venice, where they were brought by the crusaders in the thirteenth century. (The famous porphyry statues of Late Roman emperors, also transferred from Constantinople and placed at the entrance to the palace of the Doge, appear at the corner). Fragments of identical capitals and columns have recently been brought to light by the excavation of the church of Saint Polykleutos, which was erected in the early sixth century and abandoned around AD 1000.

has been embodied in the form of preserved sources, documents and results, which in every generation have to be 'read' afresh—and have not concerned myself with archaeology's future.

As I see it the man-made material reality, or the world from the earliest times until today, is what the full potential of archaeology consists of—and this is valid whether the material is found in the earth or not. Perhaps the part of the material reality which surrounds us in the immediate present and in the only slightly more distant ones will be drawn more closely into the considerations and studies of archaeology, but of course one cannot know if that will be the case. Even such general aspects can only be dealt with pragmatically in a present and subjective perspective, coloured by one's own experience.

The future must therefore wait until it becomes the present. We ourselves cannot wait; the possibilities are too numerous, the challenges too large. Night strolls in Venice and other quests or calm pleasures may soothe the soul, but they do not satisfy it until day comes, bringing work and more small puzzle-pieces which history adds to the picture of itself, and more small pieces which again vanish.

The last paraphrases: Archaeology is like a journey by a deaf person to a foreign land—the kingdom of the eye, the sense of touch and the brain. The archaeologist is like a tourist who does not speak the language. The archaeological reality is like old photographs or a damaged film with the unknown and the recognisable mixed together. The recognisable illuminates the unknown, and the unknown changes the recognisable. In the reality of the present moment, where all the senses are alive, all information is available and all is possible, the returned traveller can raise his glance—richer and perhaps also wiser. The words and the message to others about the journey can travel from the brain to the hands, to the computer, while the plant above imperceptibly grows.

ARCHAEOLOGY AND THE MAN-MADE MATERIAL REALITY

Fig. 27. Column inspired by late Antique capitals (like the ones from Constantinople/Venice in fig. 26) from the Jesus Church, Copenhagen, built at the end of the nineteenth century. An example of highly conscious imitation on an eclectic piece of architecture sponsored by the Jacobsen family of brewers, who were also the creators of the famous Carlsberg Foundation, the New Carlsberg Glyptotheque, etc.

This church constitutes an interesting case of the uses of the material culture of past traditions to create an impressive symbol in a later age of social and economic change. Incidentally, the bell-tower, unique in Copenhagen, is modelled on the famous *campanile* of San Marco in Venice.

Bibliography

This bibliography consists mainly of introductions to archaeology, general and thematic studies, characteristic analyses, collections of data, and works on the history of the subject. Nearly all references are briefly annotated and are intended to serve as intellectual thresholds between the text and the problems and specific examples discussed. No attempt has been made to cover any subject in full; the works have been included for their quality and relevance—and because of their importance in the present context.

The bibliography is followed by specific references to individual chapters and by a short list of selected major periodicals. An asterisk (*) indicates that a work is introductory or of general scope, and not always included in the chapter references, or in the captions.

R. McC. Adams: *Heartland of Cities: Surveys of Ancient Settlement and Land Use of the Central Floodplain of the Euphrates*, Chicago (University of Chicago Press) 1981. (Neo-classic investigation of settlement changes in one of the most important regions of the world.)

P. Bennike: *Palaeopathology of Danish Skeletons, A Comparative Study of Demography, Disease and Injury*, Copenhagen (Akademisk Forlag) 1985. (Health in prehistory, the case of Denmark.)

J. Berglund: Kirkebjerget—A Late Bronze Age Settlement at Voldtofte, South-West Funen. An Interim Report on the Excavations of 1976 and 1977, *Journal of Danish Archaeology* 1, 1982, 51ff. (Excavations at a Bronze Age chieftain's centre.)

*S.R. Binford & L.R. Binford (eds.): *New Perspectives in Archeology*, Chicago (Aldine) 1968. (A classic in recent archaeology for its suggestions of interpretation.)

N. Björnhem & U. Säfvestad: *Fosie IV, Byggnadstradition och bosättningsmönster*, Malmöfund 5, 1989. (Settlement analysis.)

*J.H.F. Bloemers, L.P. Louwe Kooijmans & H. Safatij: *Verleden Land, Archeologische opgravingen in Nederland*, Amsterdam (Meulenhoff Informatief) 1981. (Model introduction and survey.)

*G. Burenhult, (E. Baudou & M.P. Malmer): *Länkar till vår forntid - en introduktion i Sveriges arkeologi*, Stockholm (Bra Böcker) 1988. (Good introduction to archaeology in Sweden.)

D. Carlsson: Mellan karta och fornlämning, Trender och traditioner i kulturlandskapsforskningen, in A. Andrén (ed.): *Medeltidens födelse*, Symposier på Krapperups borg 1, Krapperup (Gyllenstiernska Krapperupsstiftelsen) 1989, 25ff. (Hidden landscapes.)

*T. Champion, C. Camble, S. Shennan & A. Whittle: *Prehistoric Europe*, London (Academic Press) 1984. (Recent survey.)

*V.G. Childe: *The Dawn of European Civilization*, London (Kegan Paul, Trench, Trubner & Co.) 1925. (Classic attempt at surveying and discussing a large and complex set of data; six later revised editions.)

*V.G. Childe: *The Danube in Prehistory*, Oxford (Clarendon Press) 1929. (See Childe 1925.)

*R. Christlein: *Die Alamannen, Archäologie eines lebendiges Volkes*, Stuttgart (Theiss) 1978. (Survey and analysis of a cultural complex, and the nation of the Alamanni.)

*J.G.D. Clark: *Prehistoric Europe, The Economic Basis*, London (Methuen) 1952. (A classic in economic archaeology.)

*D.L. Clarke: *Analytical Archaeology*, London (Methuen) 1968. (A classic in recent archaeology for its systematics.)

*J.N. Coldstream: *Geometric Greece*, London (Methuen) 1979 (1977). (Characteristic high quality survey of data.)

*T. Cornell & J. Matthews: *Atlas of the Roman World*, Oxford (Phaidon) 1982. (Figures and text in symbiosis.)

*A. Cotterell (ed.): *(The Penguin Encyclopedia of) Ancient Civilizations*, London (Penguin) 1988 (1980). (Useful short survey of the ancient civilizations of the world.)

*G. Daniel: *The Idea of Prehistory*, Harmondsworth (Penguin) 1964 (1962). (A history of prehistoric archaeology.)

*J. Deetz: *In small Things Forgotten, The Archaeology of Early American Life*, Garden City (Anchor Press) 1977. (Archaeology of the pre-modern period.)

G. Digerfeldt & S. Welinder: The Prehistoric Cultural Landscape in South-West Sweden, *Acta Archaeologica* 58, 1987, 127ff. (Cultural interpretation of pollen diagrams.)

P. Donat: *Haus, Hof und Dorf in Mitteleuropa vom 7. bis 12. Jahrhundert, Archäologische Beiträge zur Entwicklung und Struktur der bäuerlichen Siedlung*, Schriften zur Ur- und Frühgeschichte 33, 1980. (Settlement archaeology.)

*H.J. Eggers: *Einführung in die Vorgeschichte*, München (Piper Verlag) 1959. (Excellent, somewhat old-fashioned introduction.)

*K.V. Flannery: *The Early Mesoamerican Village*, New York (Academic) 1976. (Archaeological analyses and humoristic discussion of methods.)

*C. Flon (ed.): *Le Grand Atlas de l'archéologie*, Paris (Encyclopædia Universalis) 1985. (Excellent illustrated world archaeology; in English as *The World Atlas of Archaeology*, London (Mitchell Beazley) 1985.)

R. Francovich & R. Parenti (eds.): *Rocca San Silvestro e Campiglia, Prima Indagini archaeologiche*, Quaderni dell'insegnamento di archeologia medievale della facoltà di lettere e filosofia dell'Università di Siena 8, 1987. (Complete excavation of a medieval mining village.)

H. Grimm: Informationsgewinn am Skelett: Anthropologie und Medizin als Hilfswissenschaften der Archäologie, in J. Herrman (et al.) (ed(s).): *Archäologie als Geschichtswissenschaft, Studien und Untersuchungen* (= K.-H. Otto Festschrift), Schriften zur Ur- und Frühgeschichte 30, 1977, 493ff. (Physical anthropology.)

W. Haarnagel: *Die Grabung Feddersen Wierde: Methode, Hausbau, Siedlung und Wirtschaftformen sowie Socialstruktur*, Feddersen Wierde 2, Wiesbaden (Franz Steiner), 1979. (A most important recent settlement-excavation.)

*N. Hannestad: *Roman Art and Imperial Policy*, Jutland Archaeological Society Publications XIX. Aarhus (Aarhus UP) 1986. (Archaeology of art and politics.)

*(L. Hedeager & K. Kristiansen (eds.):) *Arkæologi Leksikon*, København (Politiken) 1985. (Denmark again, introductory notes on various subjects.)

*M. Henig (ed.): *A Handbook of Roman Art, A Survey of the Visual*

ARCHAEOLOGY AND THE MAN-MADE MATERIAL REALITY

Arts of the Roman World, Oxford (Phaidon) 1983. (Roman art and applied crafts.)

*J. Herrmann (ed.): *Die Slawen in Deutschland, Geschichte und Kultur der slawischen Stämme westlich von Oder und Neisse vom 6. bis 12. Jahrhundert. Ein Handbuch*, Berlin (Akademie-Verlag) 1985 (new ed.). (Interesting, marxist integration of archaeological and other sources.)

(J. Hertz et al. (eds.)): *Danmarks længste udgravning, Arkæologi på naturgassens vej 1979-86*, Herning (Poul Kristensens Forlag) 1987. (A unique publication of all finds from the archaeological investigations in connection with the construction of Denmark's network of major gas pipelines.)

C.F.W. Higham: The Economy of Iron Age Vejleby (Denmark), *Acta Archaeologica* 38, 1967, 222ff. (Analysis of subsistence.)

*I. Hodder: *The Present Past, An Introduction to Anthropology for Archaeologists*, London (Batsford) 1982. (On the meaning of material culture.)

R. Hodges & D. Whitehouse: *Mohammed, Charlemagne & the Origins of Europe, Archaeology and the Pirenne thesis*, London (Duckworth) 1983. (Interesting attempt at using archaeological data in mega-history.)

*R. Hodges: *The Anglo-Saxon Achievement, Archaeology & the beginnings of English society*, London (Duckworth) 1989. (Early Western Europe, a regional study.)

W. Hoepfner & E.-L. Schwandner: *Haus und Stadt im klassischen Griechenland (Deutsches Archäologisches Institut Architekturreferat), Wohnen in der klassischen Polis* I, (Deutscher Kunstverlag) 1986. (Impressive architectural study and presentation.)

S. Hvass: The Development of a Settlement Through the First Millennium AD. *Journal of Danish Archaeology* 2, 1983, 120ff.

S. Hvass: Eine Dorfsiedlung während des 1. Jahrtausends n.Chr. in Mitteljütland, Dänemark, *Berichte der römisch-germanische Kommission* 67, 1986, 529ff. (Survey of an important archaeological site.)

Å. Hyenstrand: *Arkeologisk regionalindelning av Sverige*, Stockholm (Riksantikvarieämbetet) 1979. (Ancient monuments, regional distribution patterns.)

*J. Jensen: *The Prehistory of Denmark*, London (Methuen) 1982.

(Recent introduction to a still expanding archaeological tradition.)

*P. Johnstone: *The Sea-craft of Prehistory*, London (Routledge & Kegan Paul) 1980. (The ship in archaeology and early history.)

L. Jørgensen: Family Burial Pratices and Inheritance Systems, The Development of an Iron Age Society from 500 BC to AD 1000 on Bornholm, Denmark, *Acta Archaeologica* 58, 1987, 17ff. (Graves and the small society.)

*L. Karlsson: *Nordisk form, om djurornamentik*, The Museum of National Antiquities, Stockholm, Studies 3, 1983. (Survey of animal art.)

F. Kaul: Sandagergård, A Late Bronze Age Cultic Building with Rock Carvings and Menhirs from Northern Zealand, Denmark, *Acta Archaeologica* 56, 1985, 31ff. (Important survey find.)

K. Kristiansen (ed.): *Archaeological Formation Processes, The representativity of archaeological remains from Danish Prehistory*, København (Nationalmuseet) 1985. (Source evaluations.)

*P. Levi: *Atlas of the Greek World*, Oxford (Phaidon) 1984. (Figures and text.)

*S. Lloyd: *The Archaeology of Mesopotamia, from the Old Stone Age to the Persian Conquest*, London (Thames & Hudson) 1978. (Fine, detailed survey.)

*I. Longworth & J. Cherry (eds.): *Archaeology in Britain since 1945, New Directions*, London (British Museum) 1986. (Nationwide review of research.)

G. Magnusson: *Lågteknisk järnhantering i Jämtlands län*, Jernkontorets Bergshistoriska Skriftserie 22, Stockholm 1986. (Study of the development of iron technology and its historical implications.)

*D.L. Mahler, C. Paludan-Müller & S. Stummann Hansen: *Om Arkæologi, Forskning, formidling, forvaltning - for hvem?* København (Reitzel) 1983. (Thought-provoking 'angry young men'.)

*C.-A. Moberg: *Introduktion till Arkeologi, Jämförande och nordisk fornkundskap*, Stockholm (Natur och Kultur) 1969. (Intellectual introduction; translated into a number of languages.)

*W. Müller-Wiener: *Bildlexikon zur Topographie Istanbuls, Byzantion-Konstantinupolis-Istanbul bis zum Beginn des 17. Jahrhunderts*, Tübingen (Wasmuth) 1977. (A model presentation of the historical monuments of a whole city.)

ARCHAEOLOGY AND THE MAN-MADE MATERIAL REALITY

B. Myhre: Settlements of southwest Norway during the Roman and Migration periods, *Offa* 39, 1982. 197ff. (Important settlement data.)

U. Møhl: Vejleby-fundets dyreknogler, *Lolland-Falsters Stiftsmuseum* 1971, 17ff. (Analysis of animal bone-refuse.)

I. Nielsen (ed.): *Bevar din arv, 1937 - Danmarks fortidsminder - 1987*, København (Gad) 1987. (Protection of ancient monuments in Denmark—and administrative archaeology.)

G. Nyegaard: Faunalevn fra yngre stenalder på øerne Syd for Fyn, in J. Skaarup: *Yngre stenalder på øerne syd for Fyn*, Rudkøbing (Langelands Museum) 1985, 426ff. (Analyses of animal bone-refuse and subsistence.)

(C. Osterwalder & P.-A. Schwarz (eds.):) *Chronologie, Archäologische Daten der Schweiz*, Antiqua 15 (Veröffentlichung der Schweizerischen Gesellschaft für Ur- und Frühgeschichte), 1986. (Important work on C-14 and dendrochronological dates.)

*L. Pauli: *Die Alpen in Frühzeit und Mittelalter*, München (C.H. Beck) 1980. (Regional approach; in English as *The Alps, Archaeology and Early History*, London (Thames and Hudson) 1984.)

R. Perini: *Scavi archeologici nella palafitticola di Fiavé-Carera I, Campagne 1969-1976, Situazione dei depositi e dei resti strutturali*, Patrimonio storico del Trentino 8, Trento (Servizio Beni Culturali della Provincia Autonoma di Trento) 1984.

R. Perini: *Scavi archeologici nella zona palafitticola di Fiavé-Carera II, Campagne 1969-1976, Resti della cultura materiale, Metallo - osso - litica - legno*, Patrimonio storico del Trentino 9, Trento (Servizio Beni Culturali della Provincia Autonoma di Trento) 1987.

T.W. Potter: *The Changing Landscape of South Etruria*, London (Paul Elek) 1979. (Early attempt at an archaeological history of landscape.)

*P. Rahtz: *Invitation to Archaeology*, Oxford (Blackwell) 1985. (Humoristic, but thorough introduction.)

K. Randsborg: Social Stratification in Early Bronze Age Denmark: a Study in the Regulation of Cultural Systems, *Prähistorische Zeitschrift* 49; 1, 1974, 38ff. (Early study of Bronze Age society.)

*K. Randsborg: *The Viking Age in Denmark*, The Formation of a State, London/New York (Duckworth/St. Martin's) 1980. (The Viking period in the light of modern archaeology.)

K. Randsborg: Women in Prehistory: The Danish Example, *Acta Archaeologica* 55, 1984, 143ff. (The role and status of women, a regional study.)

K. Randsborg & C. Nybo: The Coffin and the Sun, Demography and Ideology in Scandinavian Prehistory, *Acta Archaeologica* 55, 1984, 161ff. (Prehistoric world views and rituals.)

K. Randsborg: Subsistence and Settlement in Northern Temperate Europe in the First Millennium A.D., in G. Barker & C. Gamble (eds.): *Beyond Domestication in Prehistoric Europe, Investigations in Subsistence Archaeology and Social Complexity*, London (Academic) 1985, 233ff. (A survey of archaeological basics.)

K. Randsborg (ed.): *The Birth of Europe, Archaeology and Social Development in the First Millennium A.D.*, Analecta Romana Instituti Danici, Supplementum XVI, 1989 (I). (Papers from international symposium.)

K. Randsborg: Archaeology in the Twentieth Century: A Scandinavian View, *Acta Archaeologica* 60, 1989 (II), 151ff. (History and politics of archaeology.)

K. Randsborg: The Metamorphosis of Antiquity, Centre and Periphery in Europe from One Thousand Years BC to One Thousands Years AD, *Acta Archaeologica* 60, 1989 (III), 165ff. (Integrated Europe in Antiquity and the early Middle Ages.)

K. Randsborg: Between Italy and Afghanistan, Archaeological Surveys and Ancient Civilizations, *Acta Archaeologica* 60, 1989 (IV), 175ff. (The "evil empires", archaeology and landscape history.)

K. Randsborg: Beyond the Roman Empire, Archaeological Discoveries in Gudme of Funen, Denmark, *Oxford Journal of Archaeology* 9;3, 1990, 355ff. (A Royal centre and emporium from the early first millennium AD.)

K. Randsborg: Gallemose, A Chariot from the Early Second Millennium BC in Denmark? *Acta Archaeologica* 62, 1991 (I), 109ff. (Early international communication.)

*K. Randsborg: *The First Millennium A.D. in Europe and the Mediterranean, An Archaeological Essay*, Cambridge (Cambridge University Press) 1991 (II). (Archaeology and its contribution to megahistory.)

*C. Renfrew: *The Emergence of Civilisation, The Cyclades and the*

Aegean in the Third Millennium B.C., London (Methuen) 1972. (A social approach to the Aegean Bronze Age.)

*C. Renfrew: *Archaeology and Language, The Puzzle of Indo-European Origins*, London (Penguin) 1989 (1987). (Interesting archaeological approach to a major historical and linguistic problem.)

C. Renfrew & P. Bahn: *Archaeology—Theories, Methods, and Practice*, London (Thames and Hudson) 1991. (A monumental new Anglo-American introduction; will it be read in Samarkand?)

C. Renfrew, J.E. Dixon & J.R. Cann: Further Analysis of Near Eastern Obsidians, *Proceedings of the Prehistoric Society* N.S. XXXIV, 1968 319ff. (Classic presentation of early trading patterns.)

C. Renfrew & M. Wagstaff (eds.): *An Island Polity, The archaeology of exploitation in Melos*, Cambridge (Cambridge University Press) 1982. (Excellent attempt at a general study of all sources concerning a small region.)

*G. Richter: *A Handbook of Greek Art, A Survey of the Visual Arts of Ancient Greece*, London (Phaidon) 1959. (A neo-classic in classical art-archaeology.)

*S.A. Semenov: *Prehistoric Technology, an Experimental Study of the oldest Tools and Artefacts from Traces of Manufacture and Wear*, Bath (Adams & Dart) 1964; original Russian edition 1957. (A classic in the study of Stone Age technology.)

*M. Shanks & C. Tilley: *Re-Constructing Archaeology*, Cambridge (Cambridge University Press) 1987. (New philosophy, theory, practice; and archaeology as a tool of the mind.)

A.G. Sherratt: Plough and pastoralism: aspects of the secondary products revolution, in I. Hodder, G. Isaac & N. Hammond (eds.): *Pattern of the Past: Studies in honour of David Clarke*, Cambridge (Cambridge University Press) 1981, 261ff. (The stages of neolithization.)

*A. Sherratt (ed.): *The Cambridge Encyclopedia of Archaeology*, Cambridge (Cambridge University Press) 1980. (Short intelligent introductions to the themes of world archaeology.)

B. Skar & S. Coulson: The Early Mesolithic Site Rørmyr II, A Re-examination of one of the Høgnipen Sites, SE Norway, *Acta Archaeology* 56, 1985, 167ff. (Reversing the process of flint-knapping.)

*A.M. Snodgrass: *Archaic Greece: the age of experiment*, London (Dent) 1980. (Archaeology and some history.)

P. Stehli: Merzbachtal—Umwelt und Geschichte einer bandkeramischen Siedlungskammer, *Germania* 67, 1989, 51ff. (Summary analysis of one of the components of the Altenhovener project.)

C. Strahm (et al.): Zur Einführung, Das Forschungsvorhaben: 'Siedlungsarchäologische Untersuchungen im Alpenvorland' (and other papers), *Archäologische Nachrichten aus Baden* 38/39, 1987, 4ff. (Reports from important settlement investigations in Southern Germany.)

*D.H. Thomas: *Archaeology*, New York (Holt, Rinehart and Winston) 1979. (A heavy presentation of American points of view.)

(C.J. Thomas:) *Ledetraad til Nordisk Oldkyndighed*, Kjøbenhavn (Det kongelige Nordiske Oldskriftselskab) 1836. (The classical presentation of the three-age system, etc.; also in English and German.)

*B.G. Trigger, B.J. Kemp, D. O'Connor & A.B. Lloyd: *Ancient Egypt, A Social History*, Cambridge (Cambridge University Press) 1983. (Interesting survey; powerful written sources.)

*E.R. Wolf: *Europe and the People without History*, Berkeley (University of California Press) 1982. (Historical interpretations with methodological consequences for archaeologists.)

J.J.A. Worsaae: *Danmarks Oldtid oplyst ved Oldsager og Gravhøie*, Kjøbenhavn (Selskabet for Trykkefrihedens rette Brug) 1843. (The earliest modern archaeological work; also in English.)

Specific References

Chapter 1: Deetz 1977 (insights into material data).

Chapter 2: Daniel 1964 (history of archaeology); (Thomsen) 1836 (three-period system); Eggers 1959 (chronology in general); (Osterwalder & Schwatz) 1986 (C-14 & dendro-chronology).

Chapter 3: Childe 1925, and Childe 1929 (cultures in European prehistory); Daniel 1964 (history of archaeology); Renfrew, Dixon &

Cann 1968 (obsidian); Donat 1980 with Randsborg 1985 (Germans and Slavs).

Chapter 4: Worsaae 1843 (foundations of prehistoric archaeology); Daniel 1964 (history of archaeology); Champion, Gamble, Shennan & Whittle 1984 (early man); Clark 1952 (early economic studies); Digerfeldt & Welinder 1987 (pollen analyses); Bennike 1985, and Grimm 1977 (health); Randsborg 1984 (women in prehistory); Hvass 1986 (Vorbasse); Haarnagel 1979 (Feddersen Wierde); Francovich & Parenti 1987 (Rocca San Silvestro); Randsborg 1991 (surveys); Kristiansen 1985 (representativeness of sources); Renfrew & Wagstaff 1982 (Melos); Adams 1981 (Mesopotamia); Myhre 1982 (Norwegian settlements); Stehli 1989 (settlements on the Altenhovener Platte); Strahm (et al.) 1987 (settlements in southern Germany); Perini 1984, and 1987 (settlement site in northern Italy).

Chapter 5: Hodder 1982, and Shanks & Tilley 1987 (material culture); Jørgensen 1987 (family graves, Bornholm); Randsborg 1974, and Randsborg & Nybo 1984 (Bronze Age graves); Hvass 1986 (Vorbasse); Randsborg 1990 (Gudme-Lundeborg); Randsborg 1991 (II) (aesthetics, etc.); Karlsson 1983 (Germanic animal art); Christlein 1978 (German warrior elites, etc.); Hannestad 1986 (Roman portraits).

Chapter 6: Randsborg 1980, and 1991 (II) and Hodges 1989, and Hodges & Whitehouse 1983 (archaeology and history); Randsborg 1991 (II) (the first millennium AD, the fall of the Roman Empire); Randsborg 1989 (vikings); Sherratt 1980, and Champion, Gamble, Shennan & Whittle 1984 (Neolithic, Bronze and Iron Age Europe); Sherratt 1981 (stages of neolitization); Randsborg 1991 (I) (chariots); Cotterell 1988, and Randsborg 1989 (IV) (ancient civilizations); Randsborg 1989 (III) (developments during the first millennium BC).

Chapter 7: Nielsen (ed.) 1987 (cultural heritage); Randsborg 1989 (II) (archaeology in the twentieth century).

Chapter 8: Randsborg 1991 (II) (San Marco, Venice).

Periodicals

The following twenty (or rather, twenty-two) periodicals are selected for their quality, importance and relevance for various archaeological disciplines, traditiones, trends and activities, as well as for their characterization of the archaeological practice of different, mainly European, areas. A personal, general archaeological and northern European perspective may be noted in the selection. Some journals are rather conservative, analytical rather than interpretative, others stand in the forefront of current debates and presentations of new finds. All of them serve as references to further periodicals and other publications.

Many periodicals have been omitted; thus, the list only makes up a tiny sample of the colosal number of good archaeological journals and series of monographs available today, many highly specialized and with an enthusiastic circle of readers. The periodicals covering more than one country (or area) are marked with an asterisk (*).

1 * *Acta Archaeologica* (Copenhagen)
2   *Acta Archaeologica (Hungaria)* (Budapest)
3 * *American Journal of Archaeology* (Boston)
4 * *American Antiquity* (Washington)
5   *Annual of the British School at Athens* (London)
6 * *Antiquity* (Cambridge)
7   *Archeologia Mediavale* (Siena)
8   *Archeologia Polona* (Wrocław)
9 (*) *Archäologisches Korrespondenzblatt* (Mainz)
10   *Berichten van de Rijksdienst voor het Oudheidkundig Bodemonderzoek* (Amersfoort)
11 * *Bulletin of the American Schools of Oriental Research* (Jerusalem/Baghdad)
12   *Fundberichte aus Baden-Württemberg* (Stuttgart)
13   (a) *Gallia* & (b) *Gallia Préhistoire* (Paris)
14 (*) *Germania* (Frankfurt a.M.)
15   *Jahrbuch der schweizerischen Gesellschaft für Ur- und Frühgeschichte* (Basle)
16   *Medieval Archaeology* (London)

17   *Mélanges de l'École française de Rome*, (a) *Antiquité*; (b) *Moyen âge* (Rome)
18   *Slovenská Archeológia* (Nitra)
19 (*) *Sovjetskaja Archeologija* (Moscow)
20 * *World Archaeology* (London)

Among the very many archaeological series of monographs only one will be mentioned here, the highly productive and interesting *BAR (British Archaelogical Reports) International Series* (Oxford), which gives a good overview of current themes and subjects of study; many of the volumes are theses and conference reports. The quality of this series is somewhat uneven, however, and lately it has slowed down production. *Oxbow Monographs in Archaeology* (Oxford) may become the successor.

A number of high quality popular archaeological magazines (often glossy) are also available. One af the most remarkable is perhaps *Skalk* (Højbjerg) which has one per cent of the entire population of Denmark as subscribers.

Index